Praise for *The Traveler's Gift*

"I could not put this book down. The story itself is gripping, and the wisdom is for the ages."

—Thurl "Big T" Bailey, Musician and Former NBA Star

"Andy Andrews brings his message of success in an inspiring, entertaining, and most intriguing way. I couldn't put it down. I needed to know where it would take me, how it would end. The dialog flows smoothly and naturally; the people are very real. The historic examples are captivating; they connect with a reader's experiences and knowledge."

—Peter Boespflug, Director of Communications,
New York State United Teachers

"In this day of constant bombardment by spiritual junk food, mental detours, and outright immorality, it's refreshing to come across something that is nourishing, substantive, and inspiring. Thank you, Andy Andrews!!"

—Pat Boone, Entertainer

"It's rare to find a book that you just don't want to end, where you savor each page, reading slower as the book nears completion. The incredibly insightful seven decisions of success and Andy's enchanting storytelling abilities make The Traveler's Gift *one of those rare few."*

—Scott Jeffrey, Author of *Journey to the Impossible*

"Andy Andrews has an obvious charming talent for weaving a compelling story with characters both familiar and impressive. The Traveler's Gift *touched me in a way no other book ever has."*

—Barbara Johnson, Humorist and Bestselling Author
of *Stick a Geranium in Your Hat and Be Happy*

"The Traveler's Gift *is extremely powerful. It's helping me with things in both my personal and professional life. It's made a truly positive impact—I have no doubt that it will touch many, many lives."*

—Theresa Reagan, Executive Director,
　Children's Health Education Center

"In this short and powerful book, Andy uses a story to drive home important advice to any person seeking a better way. From the lips of one of our greatest presidents comes the type of advice that you've always needed to hear—but never took the time to listen to. You'll gain wisdom in only a few hours from this book!"

—Tim Sanders, Chief Solutions Officer for Yahoo! and Author of
　Love is the Killer App: How to Win Business and Influence Friends

"The Traveler's Gift *provides a powerful and compelling road map through the highways of life."*

—John Schuerholz, General Manager, Atlanta Braves

"A fresh approach to changing your thinking! The Traveler's Gift *will encourage you to live up to your fullest potential."*

—Dr. Robert Schuller, Founder, The Crystal Cathedral

"I was spellbound. Andy Andrews captured my heart with The Traveler's Gift."

—Gary Smalley, Author and Speaker

"Andy Andrews' book, The Traveler's Gift, *gives support to something I have believed for a very long time: The principles that underlie success have not changed in over 6,000 years! Andrews' book is worth reading; it will engage your mind and inspire your heart."*

—Hyrum W. Smith,
　Co-Chairman of the Board, FranklinCovey

THE TRAVELER'S GIFT

*Seven Decisions That
Determine Personal Success*

✦

ANDY ANDREWS

W PUBLISHING GROUP

AN IMPRINT OF THOMAS NELSON

Published in Nashville, Tennessee, by W Publishing Group, an imprint of Thomas Nelson.

Thomas Nelson titles may be purchased in bulk for educational, business, fund-raising, or sales promotional use. For information, please e-mail SpecialMarkets@ThomasNelson.com.

Scripture quotations are taken from the Holy Bible, New International Version®, NIV®. © 1973, 1978, 1984 by Biblica, Inc.™ Used by permission of Zondervan. All rights reserved worldwide.

Cover design by Gearbox.

ISBN 978-0-7852-7322-6 (tp)

Library of Congress Cataloging-in-Publication Data

Andrews, Andy, 1959–
    The traveler's gift : seven decisions that determine personal success / Andy Andrews.
        p. cm.
    ISBN 978-0-7852-6428-6 (hc)
    1. Conduct of life. 2. Success. I. Title.
BJ1597 .A53 2002
813'.54—dc21   2002007835

Printed in the United States of America

19 20 21 LSC 52 51 50

Dedicated to
the memory of
my parents,
Joyce and Larry
Andrews

In great deed, something abides. On great fields, something stays. Forms change and pass, bodies disappear but spirits linger to consecrate ground for the vision place of the soul. And reverent men and women from afar and generations that know us not and that we know not of, shall come here to ponder and to dream and the power of the vision shall pass into their souls.

—JOSHUA LAWRENCE CHAMBERLAIN, 1828–1914

ONE

✛

HEADLIGHTS SWEPT THE HOUSE AS THE TAXI TURNED out of the driveway. David Ponder stood alone on his front lawn looking at the home where he and his wife, Ellen, had lived for more than twenty years. David lowered himself onto the grass. Nausea poured over him as he felt panic enter his very soul. Like a serpent easing up his spine and wrapping itself around his throat, it wasn't a quick, devastating attack, but a slow, gripping realization that life, as he knew it, was over. He was forty-six years old. He had no job. He had no money. He had no purpose.

A short time later, David stood in the doorway of his daughter's room. It had literally been a month since he'd seen her awake. Lately, his work schedule had been frantic. As a last-ditch effort to save his employer from takeover, he often left home before daylight and rarely returned until well after his family had gone to bed. Several times during the past few weeks, he had not come home at all.

David gently placed his briefcase next to the dresser and moved toward the bed. His only child's breathing seemed loud in the quiet room. Sinking to his knees, David reached out to stroke her hair. It was so soft. The Cinderella night-light she'd cherished since her fourth Christmas cast an angelic glow on her perfect face. Jennifer Christine Ponder. "My little Jenny," he murmured. David remembered the very moment she had been born . . . twelve years ago today. He glanced at the clock on the nightstand: 2:18 A.M. *Okay,* he thought disgustedly, *so it was twelve years ago yesterday.* A tear slipped down his cheek.

"David?" It was Ellen. Moving into the room, she touched his shoulder. "I thought I heard you come in. Is everything all right?"

David looked up into his wife's face. Her hair was a mess from sleeping, and of course, she had on no makeup. She wore a long white T-shirt that contrasted with her medium-length dark hair. Her brown eyes were sleepy, but she was as beautiful to him as the day they had met twenty-five years ago.

Ellen knelt beside her husband. With her fingers, she brushed the hair from his forehead.

"David," she said again, "are you all right?"

He took her hand in both of his, brought it to his lips, and said simply, "No."

⊹

At 5:00 A.M., Ellen lay asleep on her side with her head on David's chest. David was on his back, wondering how she could possibly sleep. He wasn't sure if he'd ever sleep again. For almost two hours, he'd told Ellen everything that had happened that evening.

Late that afternoon, David and a team of management personnel had gathered in the executive conference room. By five, they had begun working the phones, feverishly soliciting stockholder support. It was a desperate, last-ditch attempt to prevent a hostile buyout by a predatory conglomerate. Final notice reached the conference room shortly before midnight. Despite their best efforts—tears, pleas, prayers, and curses—the takeover had been completed. All executive and supervisory positions at the plant were terminated effective immediately.

A security guard had entered David's office less than fifteen minutes after the phone call and offered to help clean out his desk. Within the hour, David was at the guard house near the plant entrance, waiting for a taxi. After twenty-three years of service, David had been asked to relinquish the key to his office, the key to the gym, and the key to his company car.

As he lay awake, David thought about his life. He and Ellen had met the day after both graduated from Iowa State University. David had a degree in business and was determined to make his mark with a Fortune 500 company, while Ellen, with her degree in education, wanted to teach. For two years they dated. People often asked if they were brother and sister. David's height was their only difference. He, at six-foot-two, was taller than she, but the dark hair, brown eyes, and thin body type gave them a similar look.

They would have been married sooner had it not been for David's insistence on finding a career job before settling down. He worked in his father's shoe store as a stopgap measure while sending out résumés all over the country. Ellen had already been teaching fifth grade for almost a year when David was accepted as a management trainee for a chemical company in Dallas. They were married almost immediately.

David became immersed in his work. He felt that he had found a position that would allow him to be in control of his family's future. Ellen enjoyed teaching and taught right up until Jenny was born and then never went back. Financially, the family struggled a bit on one income, but it was a sacrifice they were willing to make to have one parent at home full time for their daughter.

"Ellen," David said as he squeezed her arm.

"What, honey?" she mumbled.

"Is Jenny mad at me?"

"What?" Ellen asked.

"Is Jenny mad because I missed her birthday?"

Ellen put her arms around David. "No, honey. Jenny is fine."

"*I'm* pretty mad about it, you know . . . honey . . . Ellen?"

David sighed. Ellen had already drifted back to sleep. The world could be coming to an end, and Ellen would have no problem sleeping. He never understood how she did that. She usually laughed and said she knew he'd always take care of her. *If that is true*, David thought, *how is she sleeping now? Isn't it obvious that I am failing miserably in that department?*

Staring into the darkness, David remembered walking the moonlit beach on the island of St. John. Their honeymoon to the Caribbean had been a gift from her parents. Ellen's dad owned a lawn care business and had insisted on dipping into his savings for the honor of beginning his daughter's marriage in a special way. And it was special. They walked on the beach and talked for hours. At one point, David remembered, he had taken Ellen's face in his hands and said, "I promise you everything," and she had not laughed. He had been serious, and she knew it.

For more than ten years they prayed for a child, and when Jenny came along, their lives seemed complete.

David put his energy and focus into providing a home and lifestyle in which his family would prosper. But his work at the plant, while it did provide a living, never seemed to provide a life. As David told a friend one day, "I'm working so hard to live where we want to live that I don't actually get to live there."

As the years passed, their savings were slowly depleted. A computer business David put together with an old fraternity brother was gone in two years, and rising interest rates had soured their real estate investments. Subsequently, the college fund that had been started for Jenny when she was born was used to put braces on her teeth only six months ago. David tried vainly to recall if the price he had paid the orthodontist covered everything. *Funny, the things one thinks about at a time like this*, David mused. *If I haven't already paid for having them removed, Jenny just might be wearing braces when she's thirty.*

David's mind drifted back to the beach on St. John. "I promise you everything," he had said. He felt the bile rising in his throat. David looked at Ellen, still sleeping peacefully beside him. *I promised you everything*, he thought, *and now I've provided nothing*. Quickly, David got out of bed, stumbled into the bathroom, and threw up.

Around seven, Ellen woke up alone. Putting on her housecoat and slippers, she went into the kitchen where she found her husband sitting at the breakfast table. It seemed strange to her to see him in jeans and a T-shirt. For years David had been the first one awake in their family, and by this time, he had always been ready to walk out the door in a coat and tie. It was obvious to Ellen that he had not slept at all. "Good morning, dear," she said.

"Jenny's not up yet," David said. "Coffee's made."

She looked at him for a moment. "David," she said, "everything will be fine." He turned and stared out the window into the backyard. "David," she said again, "everything is going to be okay. We've been through tough times before."

"I'm forty-six, Ellen," David said. "Forty-six-year-old executives are not being hired anywhere except McDonald's. We have a second mortgage on this house, you know. Your car is not paid for, and I don't have one anymore. I get no severance from the plant because I didn't opt out in the package deal they offered last year. We don't have any money, and I don't know where to borrow any more. This is more than a tough time, and we have *not* been through this before."

"So what are we going to do?" Ellen asked.

"I don't know," David answered. "I have no clue."

TWO

SEVEN MONTHS LATER, DAVID FELT LIKE A BEATEN man. The health insurance coverage from his former employer had run its course, and the part-time job David took at a hardware store provided little more than minimum wage. Ellen was making more money than he was. She had placed hand-printed advertisements on bulletin boards all over town and was cleaning houses five days a week. Every day for months, David continued to search for a job. The seemingly endless stream of rejections confused him. *At least I'm on my way up,* he kept telling himself. *It can't get any worse.* But it did.

That morning had dawned cold and hard. It was everything David had always hated about winter. The sky was the color of dirty water, and the below-freezing temperature, carried by a nasty wind, cut David like the thrusts of a thousand knives. Struggling into the used car he had bought with a loan from his father, David cursed at nothing and no one in particular.

The car seemed to David a constant reminder of his failure. He had answered an ad in the newspaper and paid a high school kid nine hundred dollars for what he had hoped would be temporary transportation. It was a two-door Dodge Colt, mostly faded silver except for the right fender, which was black. The brake lights quit about ten minutes after David completed the sale, and the heater had never worked in the first place.

Shivering as he drove to work, David's mind was as numb as his body. Ellen had been up most of the night with Jenny. The child had suffered with a fever and sore throat now for three days, and with the lack of sleep, none of them were feeling well. Jenny, however, was truly sick. It was the fifth or sixth time she had been ill this winter. David had lost count.

When he had gotten out of the shower that morning, he heard Ellen hanging up the phone. "Who was that?" David asked.

"It was Dr. Reed's office, David," she said. "I've got to take her in to see what's wrong. Tylenol isn't handling this."

"What kind of parent am I?" David said aloud, interrupting his reverie as he pulled the Colt into a parking place behind Marshall's Hardware. "What kind of *person* am I? What has happened to me?"

When Ellen mentioned the doctor, he blew up. Where did she think the money was coming from, he yelled, and of course, she yelled right back that she'd steal it if she had to. This was their daughter, she shouted. Didn't he care about that anymore? As David left the house, he went by Jenny's room to kiss her good-bye. She had big tears rolling down her face. Jenny had heard everything.

About ten that morning, David was loading shingles on a flatbed truck in front of the store. He was grateful for the activity. The shingles were heavy, and they gave him somewhere to focus his anger. "Ponder!" someone yelled. David looked up. It was Mr. Marshall, the owner of the store. A tall, lanky old man with curly white hair and a red nose, he was leaning out the back door, motioning to David. "Phone call," he barked as David strode past him into the warm store. "It's your wife. Make it quick. I've told you about personal calls."

"Ellen," David said as he picked up the phone. "Where are you?"

"I'm at home," she said. "We just got back from the doctor."

"What did he say?"

"David, it's her tonsils."

"Okay?"

Ellen paused. "Honey, Dr. Reed said her tonsils have to come out. He said we need to have it done right away."

"Ponder!"

David looked around. It was Mr. Marshall. "Let's go, son," he said. "I got a driver waiting on you."

"David? Are you there?" he heard Ellen ask through the phone.

"Yes. Yes, I'm here," he said. "Ellen, we have no insurance."

"I've already checked," she answered. "The operation, including the hospital, will only cost eleven hundred dollars."

David was stunned. "We don't have eleven hundred dollars," he said.

"We can put it on a credit card."

"Hey, Ponder. This is the last time I'm going to tell you. Get off the phone," the store owner warned.

David put his hand over his ear, trying to concentrate on the conversation with his wife. "We don't have any room on a credit card, Ellen. Every card is maxed out."

Ellen started to cry. "Then we'll just have to borrow the money, David. Jenny is sick."

"I know Jenny's sick, honey, but we can't borrow anything. We're a month behind on the house, two months on your car. No bank will touch us. My parents don't have any more money to loan, and God knows, yours don't. With your dad's lawn business, they struggle through the winter just to make it themselves."

Ellen could hardly talk through her tears. "Oh, David. What are we going to do?"

"Don't worry," he said. "I'll get the money somehow. Maybe I can work overtime here. Or maybe I can get an advance. I'll get the money." As Ellen continued to cry, David pleaded with her: "Honey, please calm down. I have to go. I'll take care of this, I promise. I love you." He hung up the phone.

Turning to move from behind the counter, David met Mr. Marshall face-to-face. "I'm sorry . . . ," he started to say, but the old man cut him off.

"Your next job, you need to pay attention to the rules," Marshall said.

David was confused. "Excuse me?" he asked.

"You can come back on Friday, and your check will be waiting. I'm letting you go."

"I'm . . . I'm fired?" David stammered. "I'm fired because I used the telephone?" Marshall stood there with his arms crossed. "My daughter is sick." The old man didn't say a word. David was incredulous. He pointed at the phone. "That was my wife calling because my daughter is sick." David paused, then said once more, this time in almost a whisper, "My daughter is sick." Raising and lowering his hands in a helpless gesture and shaking his head, David turned and walked slowly out the door.

Reaching the car, David fumbled for the keys and laughed. He had experienced a brief mental flash of the car not starting. "Mr. Marshall," he saw himself saying, "my car won't start. May I use your phone?" Twisting the key in the ignition, David laughed again as the car roared to life.

Obviously, he thought, *I am laughing because I am cracking up.* As David wheeled out of the hardware store parking lot, he wondered, *If I'm sane enough to recognize insanity, does that mean I'm okay after all?* He laughed again. This time he actually laughed until he cried.

Out on the interstate, David drove past the exit for home. Traffic was light, and it was only 11:15. No reason to go home and share the big news with Ellen just yet. *Ellen doesn't deserve this,* David thought. *And Jenny certainly did not choose me for a father. A year ago, I was on top of the world, and now, I can't even provide for my family.*

David pulled onto the shoulder. Bowing his head, he clasped his hands together. "Oh, God," he said aloud. "Oh, God . . ." He stopped and was silent for almost a minute. "Oh, God . . . ," he began again. After another minute, he put the Colt into gear and moved back onto the highway. *I can't even pray,* he thought.

On an impulse, David took the Grayton exit. Almost forty miles from home, he was driving to nowhere in particular. *Just like my life,* he thought, *going nowhere in particular, nowhere special. Didn't I used to think I had a purpose?* David wondered. *Wasn't I accomplishing something?*

David looked at the speedometer. It read seventy. There were no other vehicles anywhere in sight. He pressed a little harder on the accelerator. Eighty . . . eighty-five. As he flew over hills and around curves, David became oblivious to the speed. Ninety miles per hour. His thoughts were also racing at a furious pace. Ellen was still young. She was beautiful. If he weren't around, she could find someone else to take better care of her and Jenny. *I still have life insurance,* he thought. *Would they be better off without me? Would everyone be better off without me?*

Without any further conscious thought, David jammed his foot on the accelerator, pressing it down to the floorboard. The little car screamed as David gripped the steering wheel, trying to drive away from his life. With tears streaming down his face, he rolled the window down and steered into a straightaway. The freezing wind seemed to clarify his thoughts. "Why am I here?" David said aloud. "Why is this . . . why is everything happening to me?" He pounded his hand on the steering wheel, let his foot off the accelerator for a second, and then stomped it to the floor again. "Why . . . me?" he screamed. "Why me?"

At that instant, David's moment of despair intersected with an icy bridge. Covering a small stream, the bridge was no more than fifty feet long, but its sheet of black ice sent the speeding car careening into a spin. Tires screeching, David's car bounced off the guardrail as he crossed the short bridge and found himself still on the highway. He fought desperately for control as the car fishtailed from side to side and finally swerved off the road.

Many people, when faced with a life-or-death crisis, talk of seeing their past scroll before their eyes. They experience childhood, adolescence, and many years of living all in one split second. In that moment, one person might feel remorse while another gains an acceptance of the inevitable and receives a peaceful calm. David Ponder, on the other hand, had only questions in his heart as his car careened helplessly toward a giant oak tree. With his remaining conscious thought, David removed his hands from the steering wheel and raised them as fists to the sky. "Please, God!" he cried. "Why me?"

And then . . . nothing.

THREE

"PLEASE GET OFF THE FLOOR AND SIT IN THIS CHAIR."

Slowly, David opened his eyes and looked directly into the face of a man who seemed vaguely familiar. A small, older gentleman, his short almost-white hair was neatly combed, contrasting with the slightly disheveled appearance of his clothes. The sleeves of his dress shirt were rolled up at the elbows, and his red-and-black-striped tie was loosened at the collar. Atop his sharp nose sat a pair of round spectacles that were thick enough to make his clear blue eyes seem huge.

"This is a very inconvenient time for me," the man said. "Just sit right there and be very quiet." Turning quickly, he walked toward a huge hand-carved desk. Settling himself behind it and picking up a stack of papers, he grumbled, "As if I don't have enough happening right now."

Confused, David glanced around. He was sitting on a large Persian rug, his back against the wall of an ornate,

17

high-ceilinged room. Directly to his left was the hard-backed mahogany chair that had been indicated by the man who was now intently sorting papers across the room. To his right, a globe stood on a pedestal in front of an unlit fireplace.

Easing up and into the chair, David said, "I'm thirsty."

Without looking up, the man replied, "I'll get you something in a bit. For now, please be quiet."

"Where am I?" David asked.

"Look here now." The man cursed as he slammed the stack of papers down on the desk and pointed a finger at David. "I politely asked you to be quiet, and I'm expecting you to do it. You are in Potsdam, Germany, a suburb of Berlin in a free zone presently controlled by the Red army. It is Tuesday, July 24, 1945." Taking a deep breath and appearing to calm down, he reached for his work again. Separating the papers, he said, "There now, sit and chew on that for a while."

David wrinkled his brow. *I must be in a hospital*, he thought. *This is a creepy old place. And if this guy is my doctor, he has a horrible bedside manner.* Sitting absolutely still, trying to collect himself, David watched the man at the desk. *Why would he tell me I'm in Germany?* he wondered. *And the Red army thing? I must have a head injury. Is this some kind of psychiatric exam?*

He tugged at the collar of his dark blue sweatshirt.

Uncomfortably warm, David noticed a water pitcher and some glasses on a small table near a window directly across the room. He stood up and walked slowly to the water. From the corner of his eye, David saw the man behind the desk briefly glance up, frown, and go back to his work.

David quietly poured a glass of water and, drinking it, looked out the window. He was obviously in a second-floor room of this building or house or whatever it was. Below him, no more than fifty feet away, was the bank of a slow-moving river. There were no people boating, no children playing—in fact, he didn't see anyone at all. "Something isn't right here," David muttered as a breeze crossed his face and rustled the drapes beside him.

Reaching his arm through the open window, David was almost startled to find that the air was warm and humid. Then he realized what had been bothering him. It was the air itself. The air was *warm*. Every tree within sight was full of leaves, and the grass in the yard below him was green. In the dead of winter?

Putting his glass down on the table, David placed his hands on the windowsill and pushed his whole upper body through the opening. Yes, it was hot, he decided, and pulled himself back inside. *What kind of place is this?* David wondered. *Why are the windows open in the first place? As hot as it is, the air conditioning should be running full blast.*

As he moved back toward his seat, David looked around

for a thermostat. There wasn't one that he could see. The only temperature-controlling device was an old heater that someone had put in the fireplace. *Not that that heater would do anyone any good*, he thought. *It's so old, it looks like it could have been made in . . .* , David stopped in midstride. In a soft voice, he said aloud, ". . . 1945."

Wheeling suddenly, David faced the man behind the desk. The white-haired gentleman looked up and slowly pushed his work to the side. A slight smile on his thin lips, he leaned back into his chair, crossed his arms, and peered curiously at David.

David's mind raced furiously. *Potsdam . . . Potsdam . . .* , he thought. *Why is that name so familiar?* Then, like a thunderbolt, it came to him. Potsdam, Germany, he remembered from a television documentary, was the site of the famous war conference after which the decision had been made to drop the atomic bomb on Japan during World War II.

A shudder passed through his body as David put his hands to his head. *Think, think*, he commanded himself. *Who attended the war conference in Potsdam? It was Churchill, Stalin, and . . .* All the breath seemed to go out of David at once as he groped for the chair behind him. Sitting down heavily, he stared at the man in front of him. "You're Harry Truman," he said in a shocked tone.

"Yes," the man said, "I am. Though at the moment I would give anything to be almost anyone else."

Swallowing audibly, David said, "They call you 'Give 'Em Hell Harry.'"

Truman grimaced. "I never give anybody hell," he snorted. "I just tell the truth, and they think it's hell."

Removing his glasses, he rubbed his eyes and said, "Obviously, I'll not be getting any peace from this point on, so we might as well go ahead and talk." Putting his glasses back on, he rose and came out from behind the desk. "By the way," he said, "why *not* you?"

"Excuse me?" David asked.

"Why . . . not . . . you?" Looking directly into David's eyes, he enunciated the words carefully, separating them as if he were speaking to a child. "I believe that is the answer to the last question you asked before you arrived."

David frowned. Trying to remember, he said, "I was in an accident, I think."

"Yes," Truman said, "that's sometimes how this happens. And the last question a person asks is often, 'Why me?' Of course, 'Why me?' is a question great men and women have been asking themselves since time began. I know the thought has occurred to me more than once during the past few days. It's hard for me to believe that twenty-five years ago, I was a clerk in a clothing store!" Truman extended his hand and pulled David to his feet. "What's your name, son?"

"David Ponder. Am I okay?"

"Well, David Ponder, if you mean 'Am I dead?' the answer is no. If you simply mean 'Am I okay?'" Truman shrugged, "I'm not sure. I've never been given any information on how these things turn out."

Suddenly, David relaxed. Smiling, he said, "I understand. I'm dreaming, right?"

"Maybe you are," the president said, "but, David, I'm not. And even if you are dreaming, that's not a problem. For centuries, dreams have been used to communicate instruction and direction to people of purpose—great men and women. God used dreams to prepare Joseph for his future as a leader of nations. He gave battle plans to Gideon in a dream. Joan of Arc, Jacob, George Washington, Marie Curie, and the apostle Paul were all guided by their dreams."

"But I'm an ordinary guy," David said. "I'm nothing like any of the people you've mentioned—great, I mean—and I'm certainly no apostle Paul. I'm not even sure I believe in God anymore."

Truman smiled as he put a hand on David's shoulder. "That's all right, son," he said. "He believes in you."

"How can you be certain of that?" David asked.

"Because," Truman responded, "you wouldn't be here if He didn't. Occasionally, someone is chosen to travel the ages, gathering wisdom for future generations. It's as if the Almighty literally reaches down and places His hand on a shoulder, and in this particular case," the president peered over his glasses, "it was *your* shoulder."

A sharp knock at the door drew their attention. Without waiting for a response, a large, stocky man strode into the room. It was Fred Canfil, Truman's special bodyguard. Formerly the U.S. marshal from Kansas City, Fred was temporarily attached to the Secret Service and had become a favorite of the president and his family. "I'm sorry to barge in like this, sir," he said as his eyes surveyed the room. "I thought I heard you talking to someone."

"No, Fred," Truman said as he looked directly at David, "no one here." Then motioning toward the door with his hand, he said, "If you'll see that I'm not disturbed?"

"Of course, Mr. President," Canfil said as he slowly backed out, a concerned look on his face. Still glancing about, he added, "I'll be escorting you to the conference room within the hour, but if you need me before then . . ."

"You'll be right outside," Truman said as he ushered his bewildered friend from the room, "and I won't hesitate to call for you. Thank you, Fred."

As the president closed the door, David asked, "He can't see me?"

"Apparently no one can," Truman replied. "No one, that is, except the person you came to visit. Of course, that makes me look a little crazy," he said with a grin, "in here, all alone, talking to myself." Quickly, he wiped the grin off his face and continued, "But I shouldn't think anyone would find it strange. I have ample reason to be talking to myself, what with everything that's going on here." Truman cocked his head and looked at David from the corner of his eye. "It is curious how you people always seem to show up during critical points in *my* life."

"So this has happened to you before?" David asked.

"Yes," Truman said, "three times now since I became president, you being the third. The first time was the night Roosevelt died. I was all alone in the Oval Office, and this kid just appeared out of nowhere. Fred came busting through the door—almost gave me a heart attack. It was strange that no one could see him but me."

"The kid?"

"Yeah, the kid." Truman paused. "I say 'kid.' He was a teenager actually. He was having trouble deciding whether or not to finish college."

David was incredulous. "That doesn't seem to be a problem big enough for the president."

"What are you here for?" Truman asked.

"I don't know."

"Well," the president said as he moved across the room, "at least the kid had a question." Leaning against the desk, he motioned for David to sit in a chair near the globe. "Anyway, there was a lot of pressure for him to stay in school."

"What did you tell him to do?" David asked.

"I didn't tell him to do anything," Truman replied. "That's not my part in all this. I offer perspective. The ultimate outcome of anyone's life is a matter of personal choice." The president continued, "I was evidently his second visit. He had just spent an hour or so with Albert Einstein."

David shifted uncomfortably in his seat. "Will *I* be going somewhere after this?"

"Yes, you will," Truman said. "Several different places actually, but don't worry. They will be expecting you."

"So you knew I was coming?"

"I was informed as you might expect—in a dream—the other evening," Truman said. Walking around behind his desk, Truman opened the right top drawer. Removing a folded piece of paper, he handed it to David and said, "I was instructed to prepare this for you. This is the essence of why you are here. It is one of the Decisions for Success. This is the first of seven you will receive. You are to keep it with you, reading it twice daily until it is committed to your heart. For only by committing this principle to your heart will you be able to share its value with others."

David started to unfold the page. "No, no," the president said as he put his hands over David's. "Don't read it now. You must wait until our meeting is finished. As soon as you read these words, you will immediately travel to your next destination. Amazing, actually. You read the last word and—bang!—you're gone!"

David reached over and touched the globe, unconsciously turning it to the United States. "Do you know my future?" he asked.

"Nope," Truman said. "Can't help you there. And wouldn't if I could. Your future is what you decide it will be. Now you, on the other hand, could probably tell me mine." As David opened his mouth to speak, the president held out his hands as if to ward off the words. "Thanks, but no thanks. God knows, there are enough influences coming to bear without you telling me what I already did!"

"You say my future is what I decide it to be," David ventured. "I'm not sure I agree with that. My present is certainly not of my making. I worked for years to finally end up with no job, no money, and no prospects."

"David, we are all in situations of our own choosing. Our thinking creates a pathway to success or failure. By disclaiming responsibility for our present, we crush the prospect of an incredible future that might have been ours."

"I don't understand," David said.

"I am saying that outside influences are not responsible for where you are mentally, physically, spiritually, emotionally, or financially. You have chosen the pathway to your present destination. The responsibility for your situation is yours."

David stood up. "That's not true," he cried angrily. "I did a good job at the plant. I could've taken early retirement, but I stayed. I stayed to help the company remain afloat, and I was fired. It was not . . . my . . . fault!"

"Sit down," Truman said softly. Drawing a chair around to face David, who was trembling with anger and confusion, he said, "Look here, son. It is not my desire to upset you, but with the limited time we have been given together, truth will have to stand before tact."

Placing his elbows on his knees, the president leaned forward and took a deep breath. "Listen to me now. You are where you are because of your thinking. Your thinking dictates your decisions. Decisions are choices. Years ago, you chose where you would attend college. You chose your course of study. When you graduated with the degree you chose to pursue, you chose the companies to which you would send a résumé. After interviewing with the companies that responded, you chose the one for which you would work. Somewhere during that time, you chose to go to a party or a play or a ball game. There, you met a girl whom you chose to marry. Together, you chose to have a family and how large that family would be.

"When you chose the house in which you would live and the cars you would drive, you chose how much the payments would be each month. By choosing to eat rib eye steaks or hot dogs, you chose your household expenses.

And you were the one who chose not to take early retirement. You chose to stay until the bitter end. Years ago, you
began making the choices that led you to your present situation. And you walked right down the middle of the path
every step of the way."

Truman paused. He pulled out his handkerchief and
wiped his brow. David's head was hanging, his chin on his
chest. "David, look at me," the president said. David's eyes
met his. "The words *It's not my fault!* should never again
come from your mouth. The words *It's not my fault!* have
been symbolically written on the gravestones of unsuccess-
ful people ever since Eve took her first bite of the apple.
Until a person takes responsibility for where he is, there is
no basis for moving on. The bad news is that the past was in
your hands, but the good news is that the future, my friend,
is also in your hands."

As the president leaned forward to touch the younger
man on the shoulder, he was interrupted by three quick
knocks on the door. "Mr. President," came a voice from the
hallway. It was Fred Canfil.

"Five-minute warning, sir. I'll wait for you out here. Mr.
Churchill and the Russian are already making their way to
the conference room."

"Thank you, Fred." Truman chuckled. "It seems my
bodyguard doesn't care very much for Mr. Stalin. Come to

think of it, neither do I, and frankly, I keep a few of my plans to myself. But I suppose he's a necessary part of this process." He stood up and began rolling down his sleeves and buttoning the cuffs.

David saw the president's jacket hanging over the back of the desk chair and went to retrieve it.

"What will you do?" he asked.

Truman buttoned his collar, straightened his tie, and eyed David warily. "Let's not play any games here, son. I think we both know what I'm about to do. Do I want to do it? Do I want to deploy this . . . this bomb? Of course not!"

He strode to his desk and gathered several notebooks. Suddenly, he put them down again and faced David. "I don't have any idea what you know about me." He paused. "I suppose I mean that I don't know what people say about me in the . . . ahh . . ." He wiggled his left hand at David as if he could conjure up the words he wanted to say. "I don't know what they say about me where you come from. For all I know, history books are full of how I feel or how I look or what kind of scotch I drink, and frankly, I don't care. But let's get something straight between you and me. I hate this weapon, okay? I'm scared of it and concerned about what it might mean for the future of our world."

"Why have you decided to use it?" David asked the question with no accusation, no judgment in the tone of his voice. He simply wanted to understand the thoughts of this common man who had been placed in an uncommon position. "Why have you decided to drop the bomb?"

Truman took a deep breath. "I am the first president since the beginning of modern warfare to have experienced combat. During the First World War, I would have given anything, paid any price, to end the death and suffering I watched my friends endure. And now, here I sit, the commander in chief with the ability—no, the responsibility— to end this war and bring our boys home.

"Believe me," he said as he slipped on his jacket, "I have examined every option. I asked General Marshall what it would cost in lives to land on the Tokyo plain and other places in Japan. It was his opinion that such an invasion would cost at a minimum a quarter of a million American lives. And that's just the invasion. After that we would literally be forced to go house to house and take the country. Did you know that during this whole war, not one single Japanese platoon has surrendered, not one?"

David watched Truman, his jaw set, but with a weariness in his face as he placed the final papers in a leather satchel. "Yes," he said. "It must be done. How could any president face the mothers and sons and daughters of these American servicemen if, after the slaughter of an invasion of Japan, it became known that there was within the arsenal a weapon of sufficient force to end the war and it was not used?"

He stared blankly at David for a moment. It was as if he were seeing something of his own future, and it scared him. Shaking his head to clear his thoughts, he said, "Still got the paper?"

"Yes, sir," David said as he held up the folded page that had never left his hand.

"Well, then," the president said with a smile, "go ahead and read it." He walked to the door, opened it, and was about to walk through when he paused, turned, and said, "David?"

"Sir?" David answered.

"Good luck, son."

"Thank you, sir," David said.

Truman turned to leave, but again reached back in to shake David's hand. "And one more thing," he said as he raised an eyebrow, "just because I use the expression 'good luck' doesn't mean that luck actually has anything to do with where you end up." With that, the president of the United States closed the door.

All alone, David glanced around the room. He walked slowly to the desk and sat down behind it in the big leather chair where Truman had been only moments before. Carefully, he unfolded the paper and began to read.

The First Decision for Success

The buck stops here.

From this moment forward, I will accept responsibility for my past. I understand that the beginning of wisdom is to accept the responsibility for my own problems and that by accepting responsibility for my past, I free myself to move into a bigger, brighter future of my own choosing.

Never again will I blame my parents, my spouse, my boss, or other employees for my present situation. Neither my education nor lack of one, my genetics, or the circumstantial ebb and flow of everyday life will affect my future in a negative way. If I allow myself to blame these uncontrollable forces for my lack of success, I will be forever caught in a web of the past. I will look forward. I will not let my history control my destiny.

The buck stops here. I accept responsibility for my past. I am responsible for my success.

I am where I am today—mentally, physically, spiritually, emotionally, and financially—because of decisions I have made. My decisions have always been governed by my thinking. Therefore, I am where I am today—mentally, physically, spiritually, emotionally, and financially—because of how I think. Today I will begin the process of changing where I am—mentally, physically, spiritually, emotionally, and financially—by changing the way I think.

My thoughts will be constructive, never destructive. My mind will live in the solutions of the future. It will not dwell in the problems of the past. I will seek the association of those who are working and striving to bring about positive changes in the world. I will never seek comfort by associating with those who have decided to be comfortable.

When faced with the opportunity to make a decision, I will make one. I understand that God did not put in me the ability to always make right decisions. He did, however, put in me the ability to *make* a decision and then *make it right*. The rise and fall of my emotional tide will not deter me from my course. When I make a decision, I will stand behind it. My energy will go into making the decision. I will waste none on second thoughts. My life will not be an apology. It will be a statement.

The buck stops here. I control my thoughts. I control my emotions.

In the future when I am tempted to ask the question "Why me?" I will immediately counter with the answer: "Why *not* me?" Challenges are gifts, opportunities to learn. Problems are the common thread running through the lives of great men and women. In times of adversity, I will not have a problem to deal with; I will have a choice to make. My thoughts will be clear. I will make the right choice. Adversity is preparation for greatness. I will accept this preparation. Why me? Why *not* me? I will be prepared for something great!

I accept responsibility for my past. I control my thoughts. I control my emotions. I am responsible for my success.

The buck stops here.

FOUR

✛

AS DAVID READ THE FINAL WORDS ON THE PAGE, HE looked up. The office turned and seemed to shift, the edges of the room lower than its center. The desk, which had been right in front of him, appeared to stretch and curve. Standing, he pushed the chair away and stepped toward the window. He never made it. Suddenly dizzy, David felt his knees buckle, and his forward motion sent him face first to the floor. Reaching out to catch himself, David was somehow not surprised to see his hands continue through the Persian rug as if it were not there. His head, body, and legs followed into darkness.

Almost instantly, as if he had fallen through the floor into a room below, David was on his feet, alert and unharmed. He stood in a large room that was more than one hundred feet long, fifty feet wide, with a ceiling close to fifty feet high. He was caught in the middle of a group of people who were actively jostling for position in order to see a disturbance occurring somewhere to the front. The men, he could see, were bare-chested and tanned deeply from the sun. Women wore robes of brightly colored cloth, and their hair, rolled into ropes and twisted down their backs, was extremely long.

Moving with the crowd, David breathed deeply. The air smelled strongly of cedar. He noted with amazement that the walls and huge columns supporting the roof were crafted entirely from the pungent wood. The floor was fitted with massive slabs of gray, almost purple, marble.

Without warning, a gong was struck. The sound was ear shattering. Immediately, every man and woman around David ceased talking, fell to their knees, and lowered their heads. David, too stunned to do anything but stand there, suddenly had a clear view of the room.

Directly in front of him were six steps. On each side of the steps were statues of lions. Carved from dark marble, each was a masterpiece. They paled in comparison, however, to the sight at the top of the steps. Standing alone in the center of a granite pedestal was a throne made of ivory and detailed in pure gold. The back of the elaborate chair was rounded at the top and had armrests on each side. Two more lions, these made of gold, stood silent watch beside the throne.

The gong sounded again. This time, a man near the throne walked quickly to a curtain behind it and parted the

cloth. Stepping through the open space was the most radi-
ant human being David had ever seen. He wore a robe of
brilliant turquoise. Rubies and gems of every sort were sewn
into the hems and sleeves of the garment. Around his arms
and neck were bands of solid gold. The crown on his head,
also made of gold, was dusted with small diamonds. David
was open-mouthed, the only person in the room still standing, staring openly at this awe-inspiring figure.

He was a large man. In his sandaled feet, he appeared to
be slightly taller than David. His thick, dark hair was
shoulder length, parted in the middle, and seemed to be
held in place by the heavy crown. Circling to the front of
the throne, he sat down and said simply, "Let us begin."

Immediately, the crowd leaped to its feet, and the disturbance began again near the throne. As he maneuvered
to a better vantage point in order to see, David could hear
the angry voices of two women.

"He is mine!" one of them screamed.

"No, no!" cried the other. "You are a thief!"

David eased his way to the front as the crowd started to
become unruly, taking sides with the two women and
shouting insults.

"Silence," the man on the throne said forcefully, and at
once a hush passed over the people.

David moved to the edge of the steps. He was in plain
view of the two women and the throne above them. As of

yet, no one had acknowledged his presence. He felt utterly invisible. Seeing the women clearly for the first time, David noticed that one of them held a newborn baby.

Every person in the room had his eyes directed toward the throne. David felt as if he were the only one breathing. Then with a gesture of his hand, the man indicated the second woman—the woman standing alone—and said softly, "Tell me your story."

The woman bowed and said, "Your Majesty, this woman and I live in the same house. Not long ago, my baby was born at home. Three days later, her baby was born. No one was with us. Last night, while we were all asleep, she rolled over on her baby, and he died. Then while I was still asleep, she got up and took my son out of my bed and put him in her own. Then she put her dead baby next to me."

There was murmuring through the crowd as she continued, "In the morning, when I arose to feed my son, I saw that he was dead. Then I looked at him in the light, and I knew he was not my son."

"No!" the other woman shouted. "He was your son. My child is alive!"

"The dead baby is yours," yelled the woman who told the story. "You are holding my child. My baby is alive!"

David watched the women argue back and forth until the king raised his hand and silenced them all again. Carefully, the king looked into the eyes of each woman. In a measured tone, he commanded an attendant, "Bring me my sword."

David stood transfixed as the sword was brought from behind the curtain. It was very nearly five feet long—gleaming silver with a golden handle. Emeralds decorated the lower part of the shaft. The king took it in his hand, stood up, and said, "Bring the baby to me. I will cut him in half. That way each of you can have a part of him." He raised the sword as if to strike.

"Please don't kill my son!" screamed the woman standing alone. "Your Majesty, give him to her, but don't kill him!"

"Go ahead and cut him in half," the other woman snarled as she pushed the child toward the king. "Then neither of us will have the baby."

The king said softly, "I won't harm the baby. I never intended to." He pointed to the woman who was on her knees, weeping. "Give the child to her," he said. "She is his real mother."

As the woman's tears of anguish turned into tears of joy, the baby was placed in her arms, and the crowd cheered. David yelled and clapped right along with them. When the king rose from his throne, the people knelt to the ground once more, leaving David standing alone. As the king moved behind the throne toward the curtain, he paused, turned, and looked directly at David as if to say, Are you coming?

David caught the look and quickly followed him up the steps and behind the throne. Passing through the curtains, he entered a smaller but more fabulous room. Gold shields crossed with silver spears lined the walls. Pillows of linen and tanned skins were scattered in the corner near a low table covered with food of every description. Light entered the room through high windows embellished with ivory and gold.

David came fully into the center of the room. The two attendants guarding the door did not notice him, but the king, who was speaking to another man near the table, saw David and finished his conversation. "As you wish, Ahishar," David heard him say. "I am certain you, as prime minister, will make the correct decision." He moved to recline on the pillows at the table. "Please go now and instruct all the attendants to leave the hall."

The man called Ahishar was shocked. "But, Your Majesty," he said, "it is not safe to—"

"I prefer to be alone," the king interrupted. "Thank you for your concern, but at this time, it is unnecessary. Now go, Ahishar." Bowing as he left, the prime minister exited and motioned the attendants out after him.

Alone at last, David and the king stared curiously at each other. The king spoke first. "Do you know where you are?" he asked with a smile.

"Yes, sir," David answered hesitantly.

"Do you know who I am?"

"Yes, sir, I do." This time David answered the question more confidently. "You are King Solomon, sir. I recognized the story." Solomon furrowed his brow. "I mean, I recognized what happened out there." David motioned toward the curtain. "What I am trying to say is that I remember the story from when I was a child."

Solomon smiled, amused at David's confusion. "No matter," he said. "Are you hungry?"

"Yes, sir," David replied.

"Then, please, join me." Solomon pointed to an especially big pillow on which David promptly sat. "You see before you the finest food available anywhere in the world. The food, and anything else you might need, is yours for the asking."

"Thank you," David said as he reached for some fruit. "By the way, my name is David Ponder."

"Two names," Solomon noted with interest. "Incidentally, you speak my language well. Have you been schooled in Hebrew, or is your tongue also a surprise?"

"Actually," David said as he opened a pomegranate, "I was startled to find that I understood every word being spoken when I arrived. I am even more amazed that I am able to talk with you now. I never even learned Spanish, and here I am speaking effortlessly in an ancient language."

Solomon chuckled. "The dialect is not so ancient to me, my friend, but I do understand your astonishment.

Wherever you travel on this unusual journey, you will find that your mouth and ear have been granted a special ability to communicate and comprehend. This unique competence in other languages is, of course, critical to your understanding and application of the gift with which you are being entrusted."

"A gift?" David asked.

"The scrolls," Solomon answered. "I prepared this one for you only this morning." He gently placed his hand on a thin piece of leather that had been tightly wound around a small wooden rod. "It is the message that was placed in my heart for you. This is merely a part of what must be ingrained in your life before you will be able to pass the gift to others."

"How am I supposed to pass this . . . this gift to anyone?" David asked, shaking his head.

The king smiled slightly as he reached for a bunch of grapes. Plucking one from its stem, he placed it in his mouth and said thoughtfully, "That is something you may not know for yet some time. Then again, the answer could be revealed to you tomorrow. Jehovah moves mountains to create the opportunity of His choosing. It is up to you to be ready to move yourself."

David leaned forward. "I think I understand what you are saying. You mean I have to prepare for whatever is in store." Solomon nodded slowly. "Then here's a question," David said, almost sarcastically. "How do I prepare for something when I don't know (*a*) what it is or (*b*) when it will happen?" Solomon was quiet. "Sir?" David said a bit louder. He was becoming exasperated. "Look," he began again, "I'm serious. How do I prepare for an uncertain future?"

"Seek wisdom," the king said simply.

David came close to rolling his eyes. "Maybe I'm not too smart," he said, "but I'm just not catching on here. Okay, let me ask you this: How do I seek wisdom?"

"The answer I have for you will not quell your frustration with me," the king replied and then paused. "My answer is to seek wisdom."

David's mouth dropped open. He shook his head and was about to speak when Solomon interrupted.

"David," he said, "you have a condition common to most people. You hear, but you do not listen.

"Seek wisdom. *Seek* wisdom. Wisdom waits to be gathered. She cannot be bartered or sold. She is a gift for the diligent. And only the diligent will find her. The lazy man—the stupid man—never even looks. Though wisdom is available to many, she is found by few. Seek wisdom. Find her, and you will find success and contentment."

"Well," David said, "I certainly don't have success or contentment in my life right now."

"All a part of the past," Solomon noted. "Even the present is constantly becoming the past—now . . . and now . . . and now." He snapped his fingers as he talked. "The past will never change, but you can change the future by changing your actions today. It is really a very simple process. We, as humans, are always in a process of change. Therefore, we might as well guide the direction in which we change."

"How do I guide that direction?" David asked.

Solomon rose to his feet and began to walk around the room. Clasping his hands behind his back, he asked, "Do you have a child?"

"Yes, I do," David answered. "A twelve-year-old daughter."

The king said, "Are you concerned about the children with whom your daughter plays?"

"Yes," David replied. "Of course."

Solomon turned quickly and said, "You say, 'Of course.' Why?"

David wrinkled his forehead. He was trying to figure out where the king was taking this. "Well," he began, "I say, 'Of course,' because my child's friends have such an effect on her. And I mean both good and bad. We've noticed that when she is around good, respectful children, we very rarely have a problem with her behavior. But occasionally, she'll mix in with the wrong group at school, and her mother and I have to deal with the consequences at home."

"Consequences?" Solomon asked.

"Her speech patterns, her attitude, the way she dresses, how she responds to us," David struggled to find the right words. "Everything she does at her age seems to be influenced by someone else."

"How do you guide the direction in which your daughter changes?" Solomon asked.

"By keeping tabs on who her friends are," David said.

"Exactly!" the king said excitedly. "And at what age are we no longer affected by those around us? Eighteen? Twenty-one? Thirty? The answer, of course, is that we are always and forever influenced by those with whom we associate. If a man keeps company with those who curse and complain—he will soon find curses and complaints flowing like a river from his own mouth. If he spends his days with the lazy—those seeking handouts—he will soon find his finances in disarray. Many of our sorrows can be traced to relationships with the wrong people."

David got to his feet. Wiping his hands on his jeans, he said, "So this is an important step in seeking wisdom?"

"Possibly *the* most important step," Solomon responded. "Guard your associations carefully, David. Anytime you tolerate mediocrity in your choice of companions, you become more comfortable with mediocrity in your own life. If a lazy man isn't an irritation to you, it is a sign that you have accepted slothfulness as a way of life. You saw Ahishar as you entered, did you not?"

"Yes." David nodded. "I believe you said he was the prime minister."

"That is correct," the king acknowledged. "You have not met Zadok, Azariah, and Abiathar. They are my priests. Elihoreph and Ahijah are my personal assistants, Jehoshaphat is in charge of government records, and Benaiah is my army commander. All are wise and energetic men with whom I keep counsel. If it is important for a king to be careful in his choice of friends, would it not also be important for you?"

David walked to one of the gold shields on the wall and stroked it absentmindedly. "You are the wisest man in the world," he said, "and obviously the richest. Yet you said you keep counsel with those other men. Why?"

Solomon smiled patiently. "Only a fool refuses the counsel of wise men. There is safety in counsel. Sensible instruction is a life-giving fountain that will help you escape all manner of deadly traps. Find a wise man, a person who has accomplished what you wish for in your own life, and listen closely to his words." Solomon moved to the table and picked up the scroll. Placing it into a fold of his robe, he motioned to David. "Follow me," he said.

As Solomon exited the interior room, he held the curtain open for David to pass. David stepped under Solomon's arm and said, "I should be holding the curtain for you. After all, you are the king!"

Solomon laughed. "Thank you, but I appreciate the opportunity to serve *you*. When a king begins to act like a king, it is not long before someone else is king! Serving is a way we can place value on one another. A wise man is a server."

As they strode into the great hall, David indicated the throne and said, "May I touch it?"

"Certainly," Solomon replied. "You may sit in it if you wish. It is only a chair."

David placed his hands palm down on the throne. Lightly brushing the seat and armrests with his fingertips, he admired the placement of the ivory and gold. Turning, he eased himself onto the throne. Smiling sheepishly, he said, "I feel very small sitting here."

"As do I." Solomon chuckled. Then seriously, he said, "The responsibility that comes with leadership is often humbling. When I sit where you are now, I am grateful for the lessons of my father. As you might know, his name was also David. He was not only the king before me, but my mentor as well." Solomon gazed out at the empty hall, seemingly lost in thought. Continuing, he said, "My father has been dead now for many years, yet the fundamentals he taught guide me still."

Solomon removed the scroll from his garment and unrolled the skin from the wooden rod. As he passed the precious words to David, he said, "It is time for us to part, my friend. Perhaps our time together will bring more under-standing to your life's journey. I can do nothing to alleviate your struggles and would not if I were able. It is never the duty of a leader to struggle for someone else; a leader must encourage others to struggle and assure them that the struggles are worthwhile. Do battle with the challenges of your present, and you will unlock the prizes of your future."

"Thank you, Your Majesty," David said.

"Of course," Solomon replied. He smiled as he bowed slightly. "It has been an honor to assist you. Farewell." With those final words, the king walked down the steps and directly through the middle of the vast hall. As he neared the doorway at the opposite end, he clapped his hands twice. Immediately, attendants appeared to flank the king as he left the building.

Alone, David stood up and looked once more at the magnificent room. Slowly, he slid back onto the throne of King Solomon and smoothed the king's words onto his lap.

The Second Decision for Success

I will seek wisdom.

Knowing that wisdom waits to be gathered, I will actively search her out. My past can never be changed, but I can change the future by changing my actions today. I *will* change my actions today! I will train my eyes and ears to read and listen to books and recordings that bring about positive changes in my personal relationships and a greater understanding of my fellowman. No longer will I bombard my mind with materials that feed my doubts and fears. I will read and listen only to what increases my belief in myself and my future.

I will seek wisdom. I will choose my friends with care.

I am who my friends are. I speak their language, and I wear their clothes. I share their opinions and their habits. From this moment forward, I will choose to associate with people whose lives and lifestyles I admire. If I associate with chickens, I will learn to scratch at the ground and squabble over crumbs. If I associate with eagles, I will learn to soar to great heights. I am an eagle. It is my destiny to fly.

I will seek wisdom. I will listen to the counsel of wise men.

The words of a wise man are like raindrops on dry ground. They are precious and can be quickly used for immediate results. Only the blade of grass that catches a raindrop will prosper and grow. The person who ignores wise counsel is like the blade of grass untouched by the rain—soon to wither and die. When I counsel with just myself, I can make decisions only according to what I already know. By counseling with a wise man, I add his knowledge and experience to my own and dramatically increase my success.

I will seek wisdom. I will be a servant to others.

A wise man will cultivate a servant's spirit, for that particular attribute attracts people like no other. As I humbly serve others, their wisdom will be freely shared with me.

Often, the person who develops a servant's spirit becomes wealthy beyond measure. Many times, a servant has the ear of the king, and a humble servant often becomes a king, for he is the popular choice of the people. He who serves the most grows the fastest.

I will become a humble servant. I will not look for someone to open my door—I will look to open the door for someone. I will not be distressed when no one is available to help me—I will be excited when I am available to help.

I will be a servant to others. I will listen to the counsel of wise men. I will choose my friends with care.

I will seek wisdom.

FIVE

✛

I WILL SEEK WISDOM—THE LAST WORDS. THIS time, David was ready. In anticipation of the dizziness he had felt before, he closed his eyes and tensed his whole body. David could feel the skin of the scroll in his left hand as he gripped it against the armrest of the throne. He was holding on for dear life. For a moment, nothing happened. Just as David was about to relax, he opened his eyes to see his fingers literally sliding through the ivory as if it were air. The scroll was still in his possession, and David's hands, holding so tightly to a solid object only a moment before, reflexively made fists as the throne disappeared.

The next conscious moment, David was standing amid the loudest noise he had ever heard in his life. His first thought as he tried to regain his senses was *thunder*, and he looked toward the sky. Suddenly, a hand roughly slammed into his chest, grabbed his shirt, and forcefully yanked David to the ground. "Get down, man!" the owner of the hand said as he pushed David's face to the dirt. "I don't know if you can get shot, but let's not find out, okay?"

David turned his head in panic and stared at the man who had pulled him down. He was somewhere in his mid-thirties with dark brown hair and a long, bushy mustache. He wore dark blue trousers with a faded yellow stripe down the side and a shirt of indeterminate color. The clothes, like their owner, looked as if they had not been washed in a month. He was rather thin and probably tall. It was hard to tell because he was laid out on the ground firing an old rifle over a pile of rocks. The sound David had mistaken for thunder moments earlier was the sound of cannon fire.

Bullets whined off the rocks like swarms of angry bees. All around him David heard howls of anger and pain. A man not ten feet away sat propped against a tree, shrieking in agony from a wound in his stomach, while another, missing his right leg below the knee, slowly crawled toward a friend who was already dead. The cannonballs that weren't pounding groups of men found trees nearby, severing trunks as big around as the soldiers on whom they fell.

It was so loud that David had to scream to be heard. That was not a problem. In fact, at the moment, it was the most natural thing in the world—he was terrified. David grabbed at the man's shoulder and cried, "Who are you?"

The man had turned his back to the rocks where he was reloading his rifle from the muzzle. "Chamberlain!" he yelled. "Chamberlain of the Twentieth Maine!" and he turned to fire again.

Once again the man called Chamberlain turned to reload. He lay awkwardly on his side as he bit the paper from a round and rammed it down the barrel of the gun with a metal rod. "What's going on?" David hollered. "Where are we?" David had never been so scared in his life.

"Stay down!" Chamberlain yelled in reply. "No time now. We'll talk later—I hope."

David anxiously glanced around. He could see that the rocks they were crouched behind had actually been thrown up as a makeshift wall extending more than fifty yards to his right and fifty yards again to his left. They were almost at the top of a steep wooded hill that sloped down and away from them. Chamberlain continued to fire downhill, reload, and shout encouragement to the men around him.

Just beyond Chamberlain, David saw a man thrown backward, his blood arcing into the air from a wound in his throat. He landed on his hands and knees. Slowly shaking his head, he crawled toward David. Reaching the wall, he eased over onto his back, and as his arm fell across David's leg, he looked up, smiled, and died. As David stared into the unseeing eyes, he was horrified to realize the soldier was a boy, certainly no older than fifteen.

David wasn't aware of the precise moment when the shooting stopped. He had remained huddled against the rocks, looking into the dead boy's face, until Chamberlain's hand broke his trance. The man gently brushed the young soldier's eyes, closing them, and said, "Neilson. He was a good kid." He gestured to a man, obviously dead, lying across the rock wall no more than ten yards away. "That was his father. Hiram was a bank teller from Bangor. Both joined when this regiment was formed last fall. There were a thousand of us then. The three hundred that're left are strung out along this pile of rocks."

Chamberlain stood up and offered his hand to David. Helping him to his feet, he said, "I'm Colonel Chamberlain. Joshua Lawrence Chamberlain. I know why you're here, but I don't know your name."

"I'm David Ponder, sir. Is it safe to be standing up like this?"

"For the moment," Chamberlain replied as he pulled a small twig from his mustache. "But they'll sure be back. That was the fourth time they made a try for us already."

"If you don't mind me asking," David stammered, "who are *they?*"

The colonel cocked his head and frowned. "Why, Lee's boys . . . the Army of Northern Virginia. We have fully half the Confederate battle complement facing off against us in a long line that stretches to a little town about a mile that way." Chamberlain pointed with his rifle.

"What's the name of the town?" David asked.

"Gettysburg," Chamberlain offered. "Ever hear of it?"

David nodded his head as a cold boiling began deep in his stomach. "The Civil War," he whispered.

"What?" Chamberlain asked.

"I said this is the Civil War."

"Hmmph," Chamberlain snorted. "That may be what *you* call it. Stick around for a bit. I can assure you that there is nothing civil about it. Come with me," he said, beginning to walk. "We won't have much time until they hit us again."

"Joshua!" The two men turned at the shout. "Joshua!"

It was Tom and John Chamberlain, the colonel's younger brothers. Tom was a lieutenant in the regiment, while John, a muscular young man, had been pressed into service as a medic. Both were almost as tall as the colonel and wore mustaches and sideburns that almost covered their faces. They were endowed with a cheerfulness, however, that their older brother had long since discarded. "You're a little dirtier than you ought to be, Joshua, but you're looking well. Are you all right?" John asked.

"Yes. Fine to this point. You?"

"So far, so good," John said. David followed the three brothers as they walked quickly along the wall. "Sergeant Tozier was hit but not seriously. His section took some heavy losses, though."

"How're we doing, Colonel?" The question came from a

man of about fifty. He had a bandage around his head and was busily making a wounded friend comfortable.

"You're giving it to them, soldier," Chamberlain said. "Keep pouring it on." Turning to his brothers, he instructed, "John, get over the hill and find a place for the wounded. Tom, go to the rear of the regiment and see that it is well closed up. And tell the men to thin their lines. Stretch at least half the men to the left of that big rock. The Rebs are working that way, and if they flank us . . ." Chamberlain's voice trailed away. "Well," he continued, "they just can't flank us. That's all." They turned to move away when their older brother stopped them again. "Boys," he said, "I don't like this. Keep your head down. With all of us here, it could be a bad day for Mother."

As his brothers ran off, Chamberlain turned to David and motioned for him to follow. They picked their way through the broken trees and tumbled sections of the wall, stepping over the men who were preparing to fight again and the ones who would fight no more. The colonel climbed onto the big rock he had indicated earlier to his brother and helped David up beside him. "You can see them from here," he said.

David squinted through the smoke that still lay thick in the air. Following Chamberlain's gaze, he saw the gray and pale yellow uniforms of the Confederate army massing below. They were less than 150 yards away. David could see their hats and the occasional face looking up the hill.

"Who are you?" David asked.

Chamberlain had been peering intently down the hill, but at this question, he jerked his head sharply back toward his visitor. "What? I've already told you. My name is—"

"That's not what I mean," David interrupted. "I mean who *are* you? No offense, but are you famous? The other places I appeared, it was to see someone . . . well . . . famous."

Chamberlain laughed. It was a quick, dry laugh devoid of humor. "Famous? Ten months ago I was a schoolteacher. Now, I'm a soldier. For a while anyway. Actually, it was about the time I joined up that I started dreaming about you. I knew what you looked like, how tall you were." The colonel tugged at David's sleeve. "I even knew you'd be wearing this. I've never had dreams like these before. Strange, constant, every night for months. You want to hear something spooky? Just before you arrived—there in the middle of the fight—I looked up and raised my hand. You appeared. I closed my fist on your shirt and pulled you down. When I raised my hand to grab you, I knew you'd be there. It was just like in my dreams."

"Why are you here?" David asked.

Chamberlain eyed him curiously. "Do you mean the war in general or this specific desolate hill?"

"Both, I suppose."

"Hmm," Chamberlain stroked his beard. "I joined the Union army for a myriad of reasons—same as everyone else really. We got caught up in the patriotism. We were bored. We were ashamed *not* to join. We thought it'd be quick and fun. For the most part, though, I think the vast majority of our men left their homes and families because it was the right thing to do."

Chamberlain was quiet for a moment, distracted by the men forming behind fallen trees as they spread out their line. "Colonel!" one of the men yelled. "The brush is too thick here. We can't see thirty yards!"

"Dig in and stay where you are, son," Chamberlain yelled back. "They'll be a lot closer than that!"

After a few moments of silence, David prompted Chamberlain. "Colonel?" he started. "You said you joined because it was the right thing to do."

"Yes," Chamberlain continued. "Over the centuries, wars have been fought for land or women or money. Thousands of people have died in battles caused by jealousy or an insult. More than a few times, men have fought because a king or president or someone told them to fight." Chamberlain turned squarely to face David and looked him in the eye. "David Ponder, I say to you now that this is the first time in history that men have fought to set another man free. Most of us Maine boys have never even seen black skin on a man, but if it is true that all men are created equal, then we are fighting for each other. We are fighting because it is the right thing to do."

The colonel held David's eyes for a long moment, then slowly turned to look up the line of men. "I'm not certain anymore just what I expected when I signed on for this fight, but it wasn't this." He lowered himself into a squatting position, balancing easily on the balls of his feet. Picking absently at a weed that had grown through the rock, Chamberlain said, "I was at Fredericksburg, you know." It wasn't a question. It was a statement.

"Three thousand of us attacked a rock wall just like this one. We came across a field as the sun was setting. From about fifty, sixty yards they fired. We dropped in waves. Literally sheets of men falling like a curtain on a bad play. The attack failed, but I made it to the wall. I lay there all night, too scared to withdraw, cold. I burrowed down into the corpses for warmth, listening to our men shoot, their men shoot back. *Whap!* That's the sound a bullet makes when it hits a dead body. Altogether different from the sound of a bullet in living flesh."

Chamberlain shook his head forcefully as if to drive the memory away. "Oh, well," he said as he stood up. He had pulled the weed from the rock and used it as a sword, pointing again toward the wall. "That'll never happen here. This wall won't turn 'em much longer. We don't have enough men left." He threw the weed to the ground. "I have a feeling," he said, "that if we lose this fight, the war will be over."

David stepped up beside the colonel. "Why did you choose this place to defend?"

"I didn't choose it," Chamberlain said dryly. "Colonel Vincent placed me here this morning."

"Why did he place you here?" David pressed.

"We are the extreme left of the Union army. The Eighty-third Pennsylvania is formed on our right, but to our left, nothing. We are the end of a line that runs from here all the way back into Gettysburg. That means I cannot withdraw. If the Confederate army flanks us, if the Rebs overrun us, they'll come in behind our cannons and barricades, and the Army of the Potomac will be forfeit. Eighty thousand men caught from the back on a downhill charge with no protection. And if it happens, it will have come through me."

At that very second, David heard a ghostly sound resonate from down the hill. Rising to a high, thin pitch, a thousand voices strained in a long, continuous scream. It was the Rebel yell. They were coming. David caught glimpses of the soldiers through the trees as they ran up the steep hill.

Chamberlain had turned to direct David off the rock when the cannon shell hit. Striking the base of the rock on which they were standing, the projectile threw both men into the air. As he hit the ground, David felt as though a giant vacuum had sucked all the air from his body. Before he could check to see if he'd been injured—before he could even breathe—Chamberlain had him by the arm, dragging him to the protection of the wall.

Only the cannons were firing now, David realized as he struggled to get his lungs working again. He could still hear the blood-curdling yells as the Rebels worked their way up the hill. He rolled over onto his knees and glanced over the wall. They were within sight. It seemed to David as though the Confederate army was about to step into his lap. *Shoot!* he thought. *For God's sake, shoot! They're right here!*

It seemed an eternity, but finally, David heard Chamberlain call out, "Hit 'em!" A long, rolling crack of rifle fire rang out. It began near David and ran like a fuse up the line to the right. Scores of Rebels fell on the first volley. They were more careful after that, using trees to shield them from the deadly fire, but still they came.

The firing was continuous now. To David, it sounded like thunder and firecrackers thrown into an earthquake. The man next to him grunted and fell backward, his head and face a bloody mess. To David's astonishment, the man sat up, pulled a handkerchief from his pocket, and wrapped the cloth around his head. Wiping the blood from his eyes with a sleeve, he picked up his rifle and began loading it to fire again.

Chamberlain was directing his men now and had moved some distance from David. All down the line, a few of the Rebels had reached the wall. Most of the shooting was point-blank. The colonel had drawn his pistol, and David watched as Chamberlain and a Rebel, no more than three feet apart, aimed guns at each other. The Confederate soldier went down in a cloud of red mist. Chamberlain continued to fire at targets all around him until, without warning, the Rebels pulled back.

As suddenly as they had appeared, they withdrew. Chamberlain's men cautiously stood up to take stock of their situation. David walked quickly toward the colonel who was walking away from him. The rock wall, on his left side as he walked, was draped with the bodies of blue and gray. He passed a man who was crying and cursing as he held a younger man in his arms.

Jogging as he caught up with Chamberlain, David reached out and touched his shoulder. "Colonel?" he said. Chamberlain stopped, staring straight ahead. "Colonel? I know you're very busy, and I don't want to bother you, but why am I here?"

Chamberlain slowly shook his head. "I don't know. I only knew that you would come."

"There is something I am to learn from you," David pleaded. "I am sure of it. Think—what could it be?"

The colonel smiled slightly and raised his eyebrows.

Turning to David, he said, "I am a professor of rhetoric. I am fairly certain I have nothing you would care to learn. I am a teacher with a cause in my heart and men to lead. These poor men . . . their leader has no real knowledge of warfare or tactics. I am only a stubborn man, Ponder. That is my greatest advantage in this fight. I have deep within me the inability to do nothing. I may die today, but I will not die with a bullet in my back. I will *not* die in retreat. I am, at least, like the apostle Paul, who wrote, 'This one thing I do . . . I press toward the mark.'"

"Do you have anything written that you are to give me?" David asked.

For a moment, David could see that Chamberlain did not understand his question. Then recognition flared in his eyes. "Yes," he said. "I do. I had almost forgotten."

Digging into his pocket, he pulled out a small tobacco pouch. The pouch was hand-sized, navy blue, with crossed swords, the symbol of a fighting man, embroidered on the flap. It had been sewn from stout cloth, but the rough treatment it had received had worn the pouch to a mole-skin softness. The two gold buttons that closed the flap were metal, engraved with the image of an eagle. The tobacco pouch was beaten and threadbare, but it was still handsome—regal in a sense—the possession of an officer.

Chamberlain opened the pouch and extracted a small, folded piece of paper. "I wrote this more than two months ago," he said. "We've had no tobacco for longer than that, so I slipped it in here for safekeeping." Passing the paper to David, he said, "I'm a little foggy on what I actually wrote. I woke up in the middle of the night after one of those dreams. The words you have there were rumbling around in my head as plain as day. I lit the lamp, found an inkwell, and put them to paper. I knew they were for you."

"Thanks," David said as he held the paper in his hand.

"My pleasure," Chamberlain replied. "This has all been a very curious situation. By the way, how do you get out of here?"

David held up the paper. "All I have to do is read this—" he snapped his fingers, "—and I'm gone."

Chamberlain looked around him. Noticing his brother Tom and several other men approaching, he put his hand on David's shoulder, squeezed it, and said, "If that's all you have to do, then, brother, you might want to read it now."

He turned to go, then turned back to David. Still in his hand was the small tobacco pouch. Holding it out, he offered it to David. "I'll not be getting any more tobacco anyway," Chamberlain said.

Wordlessly, David took the gift and watched the colonel walk away. Alone for a moment, everything in him wanted to take Chamberlain's advice. *Read the paper now,* he told himself. *Get out of here.* But something kept nudging him to stay, to watch.

Placing the precious piece of paper back into the tobacco pouch, David shoved the whole thing in his jeans pocket and eased up to the group of men surrounding Colonel Chamberlain. Sergeant Tozier was there, the hard-nosed old soldier who carried the battle flag. Tozier had a thick wad of torn cloth stuck into a hole in his shoulder where he had been wounded earlier. "No help from the Eighty-third," he growled. "They're shot to ribbons. All they can do is extend the line a bit. We're getting murdered on the flank."

"Can we extend?" Chamberlain asked.

"There's nothing to extend, Joshua," his brother Tom answered. "Over half our men are down."

"How are we for ammunition?"

"We've been shooting a lot."

"I know we've been shooting a lot! I want to know how we're holding out."

"I'll check, sir."

As Tom moved off, a voice came from a young soldier who had climbed a tree. "They're forming again, Colonel." Chamberlain looked up to see the boy pointing downhill. "They're forming up right now," he said, "and they've been reinforced. There're more of them this time."

"Sir!" Sergeant Ruel Thomas, out of breath, stumbled into their midst. "Colonel Chamberlain, sir. Sir . . . Colonel Vincent is dead."

"Are you sure, Sergeant?"

"Yes, sir. He was shot right at the first of the fight. We were firmed up by Weed's Brigade in the front, but now Weed is dead. They moved Hazlett's Battery up top. Hazlett's dead too."

Tom came running back. "Joshua," he said, "we're out. One, two rounds per man at the most. Some of the men have nothing at all."

Chamberlain turned to a thin man standing to his right. It was First Sergeant Ellis Spear. "Spear," he said calmly, "tell the boys to take ammunition from the wounded and dead."

"Maybe we should think about pulling out, sir," Spear said cautiously.

"We will *not* be pulling out, Sergeant," Chamberlain replied grimly. "Carry out my orders, please."

"Colonel," Tozier spoke up. "Sir, we won't hold 'em again. You know we won't."

"Joshua." It was Tom speaking again. "Here they come."

David had been listening to the exchange between the officers, fascinated by the horror of their situation, but when he heard the Rebel yells coursing up through the trees once more, his blood turned icy cold. *I've waited too late to read the paper*, he thought. *I'll never get out of here now.* As he grabbed for the tobacco pouch, a calm washed over him with that same familiar urging—wait, watch, listen, learn.

Chamberlain was standing in full view on top of the wall, his arms crossed, staring down at the advancing enemy. Sergeant Spear had returned and was standing at his colonel's feet. Tozier, Tom, and another lieutenant, a boy named Melcher, were also bunched below. David stood several feet behind the group. "Joshua!" Tom shouted. "Give an order!"

Chamberlain remained stoic. Deep in thought, he was quickly sorting the situation. *We can't retreat*, he said to himself. *We can't stay here. When I am faced with the choice of doing nothing or doing something, I will always choose to act. I am a person of action.* Turning his back to the Rebels, he looked down at his men. "Fix bayonets," he said.

At first, no one moved. They simply stared at him with open mouths. "We'll have the advantage of moving downhill," Chamberlain said. "Fix bayonets now. Execute a great right wheel of the entire regiment. Swing the left first."

Lieutenant Melcher spoke up. He was confused. "Sir," he asked, "what's a great right wheel?" But the colonel had already jumped from the rocks.

Tozier answered the question. "He means to charge, son. A 'great right wheel' is an all-out charge."

David watched in awe as Chamberlain drew his sword, leaped up onto the wall again, and screamed, "Bayonets! Bayonets!" Turning, the colonel pointed the sword directly at David and slightly bowed his head. Then he wheeled to face the overwhelming odds and slashed his blade through the air. With a power born of righteousness and fear, the schoolteacher from Maine roared, "Charge! Charge! Charge!" to his men. And they did.

Tumbling over the wall, the men who were left rose their voices to meet the voice of their leader. "Charge!" they cried. "Charge! Charge!"

David rushed to the wall, looking downhill. He was stunned to see the advancing Confederate force stop in its tracks. Almost immediately, the soldiers turned and ran. A few of the braver souls emptied their rifles before dropping them to follow the rest. About seventy yards down the slope, David caught sight of Chamberlain. He had his left hand on the trunk of a tree, and in his right he held the sword, the point of which was resting on the collarbone of a Rebel officer. The man had his hands up. It was over.

David climbed over the rocks and sat down. With his back to the wall, he pulled the pouch from his pocket. As he looked down the slope, David brushed his fingers over the silky smoothness of the material. He put it close to his face and smelled the mixture of earth, sweat, and old tobacco. Unbuttoning the flap, David removed the paper that Chamberlain had written. With a final glance downhill and a deep breath, David opened the page.

THE THIRD DECISION FOR SUCCESS

I am a person of action.

Beginning today, I will create a new future by creating a new me. No longer will I dwell in a pit of despair, moaning over squandered time and lost opportunity. I can do nothing about the past. My future is immediate. I will grasp it in both hands and carry it with running feet. When I am faced with the choice of doing nothing or doing something, I will always choose to act! I seize this moment. I choose now.

I am a person of action. I am energetic. I move quickly.

Knowing that laziness is a sin, I will create a habit of lively behavior. I will walk with a spring in my step and a smile on my face. The lifeblood rushing through my veins is urging me upward and forward into activity and accomplishment. Wealth and prosperity hide from the sluggard, but rich rewards come to the person who moves quickly.

I am a person of action. I inspire others with my activity. I am a leader.

Leading is doing. To lead, I must move forward. Many people move out of the way for a person on the run; others are caught up in his wake. My activity will create a wave of success for the people who follow. My activity will be consistent. This will instill confidence in my leadership. As a leader, I have the ability to encourage and inspire others to greatness. It is true: an army of sheep led by a lion would defeat an army of lions led by a sheep!

I am a person of action. I can make a decision. I can make it now.

A person who moves neither left nor right is destined for mediocrity. When faced with a decision, many people say they are waiting for God. But I understand, in most cases, God is waiting for me! He has given me a healthy mind to gather and sort information and the courage to come to a conclusion. I am not a quivering dog, indecisive and fearful. My constitution is strong and my pathway clear. Successful people make their decisions quickly and change their minds slowly. Failures make their decisions slowly and change their minds quickly. My decisions come quickly, and they lead to victory.

I am a person of action. I am daring. I am courageous.

Fear no longer has a place in my life. For too long, fear has outweighed my desire to make things better for my family. Never again! I have exposed fear as a vapor, an impostor that never had any power over me in the first place! I do not fear opinion, gossip, or the idle chatter of monkeys, for all are the same to me. I do not fear failure, for in my life, failure is a myth. Failure exists only for the person who quits. I do not quit.

I am courageous. I am a leader. I seize this moment. I choose now.

I am a person of action.

SIX

THE NAUSEA WAS MORE PRONOUNCED THIS TIME. When the rock wall disappeared behind David's back, he immediately felt a swaying sensation drawing him down, back up, and then down again. Balling his fists and ducking his head, David wondered when the time shift would be finished. The sick feeling was almost overwhelming. Carefully, David opened his eyes and understood. The movement he had felt was not part of the travel; he had arrived in less than an instant. He was on a boat.

It was dark, but despite the darkness, David could see the water in starlight. It was the ocean, he knew, for the salty smell reminded him of vacations to the beach with Ellen and Jenny. The motion of the boat bothered him less as his vision adjusted to his surroundings. Feeling around him, David discovered that he was sitting on a large pile of coiled rope. At least he thought it was rope. It was rougher and less uniform than any rope he'd ever used. It felt as if it were made out of grass.

Touching the rope reminded David that he still held Chamberlain's paper in one hand and the tobacco pouch in the other. Excited and somewhat amazed that the pouch had come with him, David hurriedly placed the paper in the pouch and buttoned it. Then he remembered the page from Truman and King Solomon's leather scroll. Removing them from his pocket, David placed the first two priceless writings inside the colonel's tobacco pouch with the third and shoved it back into the pocket of his jeans.

Gingerly, David rose from his place of arrival. He was stiff and somewhat sore as if he'd been still for a long time. Looking up, David saw a massive broadcloth—a sail—and smiled. He had sailed with his father as a child. Small lakes and small boats—nothing this size! "Dad would really get a kick out of this," he said aloud. Then David frowned. "Where are you, Dad?" he whispered.

Suddenly, David felt very alone and very tired. Sinking down onto the pile of rope, he lay his head back as the tears welled up in his eyes. Would he ever see Ellen again? Or his daughter? Sweet Jenny. What were they thinking now? Were they scared? Happy? Had ten minutes passed . . . or a hundred years?

⟊

"My friend! Pssst! My friend!" David felt a tugging on his sleeve and opened his eyes. It was still dark, though he felt as if he'd been asleep for some time. "My friend," a figure hissed urgently, "please, if you will, come with me." After being practically jerked to his feet, David followed the outline of a small, stocky man as he lightly stepped around barrels and ropes and poles, working his way to the center of the boat.

Struggling to keep up, David almost tripped several times until, finally, the man stopped at the base of the mast. It was a large pole, bigger around than David could have reached, rising up into the darkness. Supporting the mainsail, it was covered in ropes and buckles. Without a glance at David, the man said simply, "Up," and motioned with his hand for David to follow.

The man was almost out of sight in seconds, so quickly did he climb. David hurried to keep up, but it was like crawling through a spider's web. In only a short time, however, he felt a hand grasp the back of his shirt. The small man was very strong. He heaved David up, over the lip, and into a wooden cup built around the top of the mast. They were in the crow's nest.

The man smoothed David's shirt where he had grabbed it, then placed both hands on David's shoulders. "Welcome. Welcome, my friend," he said quietly, but with enthusiasm. "I am most honored to make your acquaintance. And your name is . . . ?"

"My name is David, David Ponder."

"Ah, Señor Ponder. May I call you David?"

"Yes, of course."

"Excellent! Are you hungry?"

"No, not really. I . . ."

"Good! We have very little to eat, and what we *do* have contains wee bugs!" David flinched. "But there is no problem," the man said. "You will see. Our journey is almost at an end."

Despite the darkness, a reflection of the stars from the water illuminated the crow's nest in a soft glow. David could see the man clearly now. He had reddish-brown hair, very curly, that fell almost to his shoulders. A triangular green felt hat was set far back on his head, the forward point jutting toward the sky. The rest of his clothes, but for a stout canvas jacket, were in tatters. The man's pants fell in strips around his ankles, and his shoes were virtually nonexistent—hard leather wrapped around his feet.

"May I ask *your* name, sir?" David asked.

"Why, yes, of course." The man put a hand to his head. "How rude of me! I am Capitán Colón. Capitán Cristóbal

Colón, master of the *Santa Maria*, at your service." He gave a little bow.

"Colón?" David asked. "Columbus? You are Christopher Columbus?"

"Yes." The man smiled, a bit confused. "Columbus is the English pronunciation of my name, but your Portuguese is flawless. I naturally assumed . . ."

David grinned. "I'm speaking Portuguese tonight only."

Columbus tilted his head as if trying to understand what David thought was humorous. "I see," he said, though it was obvious to David that he did not. Clapping his hands together and rubbing them vigorously, Columbus changed the subject. "Whatever it is that you are doing tonight," he said, "the night itself will soon be over. The sun will join us shortly!"

The rocking of the vessel was more pronounced in the high perch, but otherwise, David felt safe, almost comfortable. From this elevation, he could see below that the boat was not very large compared to the vastness of the sea in which it sailed. Less than two hundred feet in length, the *Santa Maria* creaked and groaned with the rolling of the gentle waves. Looking behind her, David could just make out the shadows of two other boats. They rode the swells about a hundred yards to the rear, flanking their leader on either side.

"The *Niña* and the *Pinta?*" David asked.

"Why, yes," Columbus answered. "Seaworthy vessels both, though not quite so luxurious as this." He flung his arms out below him, indicating the deck of the *Santa Maria*.

David suppressed a smile. "Do you know where you are?" he asked.

"Certainly." Columbus smiled. "I am right here! Do you know where *you* are?"

David glanced around. "The Atlantic?"

"Good! Good!" Columbus said as he clapped David on the back. "You are a wonderful navigator!"

David was somewhat confused and more than a little uneasy. He spoke up again. "Do you *really* not know where you are?" he asked.

"Does that have any bearing on what I can accomplish?" Columbus asked in return.

"I don't quite understand," David said.

"I have heard that question in one form or another since I was a child," Columbus began. "Do you know where you are? Do you know *what* you are? Colón, you are uneducated. Colón, you are poor. You are the son of a weaver! What do you know about the sea?" He shook his head in disgust. "'Do you know where you are?' is a question that affects me not in the least! Now, 'Do you know where you are going?'— there is a question I can answer! So, ask me that."

"Excuse me? Ask you . . . ?"

"Ask me, 'Do you know where you are going?' Ask me!"

"Okay." David shrugged. "Do you know where you are going?"

For the few minutes the two men had been in the crow's nest, they had conversed in rather quiet, measured tones. At that point, however, Columbus received the question for which he had been waiting. He boomed out the answer. Carrying across the water, it sounded like the voice of God. Throwing his hand forward, pointing into the western sky, he cried, "Yes! Yes! I *know* where I am going! I am going to a new world!"

Shivers played up David's spine as he watched the explorer point into the darkness. For a moment, neither man said a word. Clearing his throat, David broke the silence. "How long since you left Spain?" he asked.

"Sixty-four days," Columbus said as he lowered his arm, "and today we shall see land. Look behind us." David turned and saw a brightening in the eastern sky. "Dawn will be breaking soon. When it does, directly in front of the *Santa Maria* you will see land. Beautiful land with trees and fruit and animals and people who will welcome us as heroes! The water gushing from the ground will be cold and pure. It will sparkle as if sprinkled with diamonds! This will be a place for men's dreams to come true—a glorious new world claimed by Cristóbal Colón in the name of King Ferdinand and Queen Isabella!"

David leaned forward and put his hands on the lip of the

crow's nest. "That would be King Ferdinand and Queen Isabella of Spain, correct?" he asked.

Columbus nodded. "They are the financiers of this expedition. King John of Portugal, *my* king, said no to this grand opportunity, as did the kings and queens of many other countries. Nineteen years, my friend. It took nineteen years to find sponsorship. For nineteen years, I endured the agony of public humiliation for my convictions."

"Which convictions?" David asked.

"The conviction . . . ," Columbus said, his voice rising, "no, the absolute certainty that I can establish a new trade route by sailing west. West!"

Columbus grabbed David by the shoulders and shook him once as he said, "My friend! The world is a sphere! It is not flat! We are sailing *around* the earth on the smooth surface of a sphere. We will not fall off some imaginary edge!"

"Are you the only person who believes this?" David asked.

"At the moment, yes," Columbus said, "but that bothers me not in the least. Truth is truth. If a thousand people believe something foolish, it is still foolish! Truth is never dependent upon consensus of opinion. I have found that it is better to be alone and acting upon the truth in my heart than to follow a gaggle of silly geese doomed to mediocrity."

"You say it doesn't bother you in the least," David said.

"You don't care that people think you are . . . well . . . crazy?"

"My friend," Columbus said with a smile, "if you worry about what other people think of you, then you will have more confidence in their opinion than you have in your own. Poor is the man whose future depends on the opinions and permission of others. Remember this, if you are afraid of criticism, you will die doing nothing!"

David frowned. "But with so many people against you," he asked, "how did you get started in the first place?"

"Getting started, getting finished—both ends of a journey require a demonstration of passion," Columbus mused. David stared blankly at the great man. "Passion!" he said again in a forceful whisper. "Passion is a product of the heart. Passion is what helps you when you have a great dream. Passion breeds conviction and turns mediocrity into excellence! Your passion will motivate others to join you in pursuit of your dream. With passion, you will overcome insurmountable obstacles. You will become unstoppable!"

David began to ask another question, but Columbus put his hand out to silence him. "Please, my friend," he said. "Quiet for a time." David did as he asked and followed his gaze into the western sky. The sun was just breaking the horizon behind them, throwing a brilliance over the miles of open ocean. Columbus peered ahead, concentrating with all his might into the distance. For one full minute he did not move. For two minutes . . . then ten. Only his eyes shifted as he scanned the line where the water touched the sky.

After almost half an hour, Columbus straightened his back and rubbed his eyes. "Nothing?" David asked softly.

"Yes, something," Columbus answered.

"What?" David looked around, confused. "You see land?"

"Yes," the great man said simply.

David frowned. He was still straining to catch a glimpse of what Columbus claimed he saw. "Point it out to me, please."

"Señor Ponder," Columbus said. "You are looking in the wrong direction. Today, you will not see land off the bow of my ship. You will see land only by looking into my eyes."

David turned. He felt as if he'd been tricked. "So there's no land?" he said indignantly.

"Yes, there is land," Columbus replied, "and it is right there." He gestured past the bow of the ship again. "I see it as plainly as I see you. For almost twenty years I have seen it. And tomorrow, you will see it too. It will come into view just as dawn breaks, directly in front of the *Santa Maria*. Beautiful land with trees and fruit and animals and people who will welcome us as heroes! The water gushing from the ground will be cold and pure. It will sparkle as if sprinkled with diamonds! This will be a place for men's dreams to come true—a glorious new world claimed by Cristóbal Colón in the name of King Ferdinand and Queen Isabella!"

For a brief time, David did not breathe. His hair rustled in the steady breeze as he looked deeply into the eyes of the man before him. He saw there the passion and belief that had fueled this voyage of destiny. *What could I accomplish,* David wondered, *with a spirit as powerful as this?*

"El Capitán!"

David blinked. The spell had been broken by a voice calling from below.

"El Capitán, sir!"

The two men peered over the edge of the crow's nest. Directly underneath them were four men. They motioned for Columbus to join them.

Columbus pursed his lips and sighed. "Trouble?" David asked.

Swinging his leg over the lip of the wooden cup, Columbus answered, "Most assuredly. These are my officers."

David climbed through the rigging, trying his best to follow the agile descent of the seaman. When at last he reached the deck of the *Santa Maria*, voices were already being raised. The first officer, though dressed exactly like his captain, was tall and heavily muscled. His long black hair had been tied into a ponytail and laid over his shoulder so that it fell down the front of his shirt. Like the other three men, he was clean shaven. Leading the contingent against their leader, First Officer Juan Garson did all the talking. "Your officers are in agreement, El Capitán. This voyage is finished! It is time to return."

Columbus looked at the men and said, "But we are almost there! The hardest part of the journey is past! Tomorrow you will see land. It will be beautiful land with trees and fruit and . . ."

"Enough!" Juan Garson cried. "We have heard this sad refrain for too many weeks. Sir, surely, you must see that the men have reached their limit!"

Columbus smiled stiffly. "I see men who don't know the limits they can reach."

Juan Garson briefly closed his eyes as if to contain himself. "Sir! Your officers and I have decided to turn back. We are at an end."

Garson and the other men moved to go but were brought up short by the booming voice of their captain. "Gentlemen!" Columbus shouted. The officers stopped and faced him. "Gentlemen," he said with less volume this time, "might I remind you that we have less than ten days of food and water left in our stores. To reverse course is the gambit of a fool. It not only means failure but certain death as well! In God's name, men, I ask you to think! We are at sea now for sixty-four days! To which port do you return? Our only course is forward! Our only hope is to press on!"

The men stood with their heads down. They seemed not

only outmaneuvered but beaten. Garson spoke again, softly this time. "Is this realistic, Capitán? Will we find land?"

Columbus moved to put his arm around the shoulders of the taller man. "Is this realistic, Garson? I say to you 'no,' but then nothing great was ever accomplished by a realistic person! Will we find land? Yes! Yes! We will find land, but that will be the least of *your* discoveries." Columbus pointed to his first officer's chest. "You will find a heart for success that you did not know existed. You will find a Juan Garson who is able to lead men to new worlds of their own! You will find . . . greatness!"

Garson straightened and breathed deeply. "Forgive my insolence, El Capitán, I . . ."

"Forgotten," Columbus said, as he made a dismissing motion with his hand. "Go, Juan Garson. Lead your men—and believe!"

As the officers left, Columbus moved once more toward the crow's nest. David followed him up, finding it easier this time because of the daylight. Again, however, Columbus pulled David into the cup by the back of his shirt.

Catching his breath, David watched Columbus settle his back against the mast and fix his gaze again upon the western horizon. "May I ask a question?" David said quietly.

"Certainly," Columbus replied.

"What did you mean down below when you told your officer that he would find a heart for success?"

Columbus inhaled and slowly blew out his breath before answering. "Most people fail at whatever they attempt because of an undecided heart. Should I? Should I not? Go forward? Go back? Success requires the emotional balance of a committed heart. When confronted with a challenge, the committed heart will search for a solution. The undecided heart searches for an escape."

Columbus cleared his throat, coughing gently, then continued. "A committed heart does not wait for conditions to be exactly right. Why? Because conditions are *never* exactly right. Indecision limits the Almighty and His ability to perform miracles in your life. He has put the vision in you—proceed! To wait, to wonder, to doubt, to be indecisive is to disobey God."

Without taking his eyes off the water, Columbus reached under his jacket and removed a parchment. "For you," he said simply. Unfolding it, he handed it to David.

David took the yellowed paper, glanced at it briefly, and said, "You *will* find your new world."

Columbus, eyes still straight ahead, spoke quietly, "I know."

David smiled and shook his head in wonder. "How do you know?" he asked.

Columbus turned and looked at David. "I have a decided heart," he said and turned back.

For a moment, David said nothing. He felt the purest

sense of awe for this man who knew nothing, yet seemed to know everything. He opened his mouth to speak again. "But how—"

"Señor Ponder," Columbus interrupted. He placed his arm over David's shoulders. "It is time for you to read the message I was given for you. Study it carefully, for it is within these words that you will find a heart for success that *you* did not know existed. You will find a David Ponder who is able to lead men to new worlds of *their* own. You will find greatness." And with those words, the great explorer Christopher Columbus hugged David and kissed him on each cheek. "Read," he said again and smiled. "I am very busy."

David watched him ease to the edge of the crow's nest, put his elbows on the lip, and look to the west once more. The wind shifted and rattled the parchment in his hand. Sitting down, David propped his back against the wall of the cup and braced his feet on the mast. Stealing one last glance at the man who had penned the words, he read.

The Fourth Decision for Success

I have a decided heart.

A wise man once said, "A journey of a thousand miles begins with a single step." Knowing this to be true, I am taking my first step today. For too long my feet have been tentative, shuffling left and right, more backward than forward as my heart gauged the direction of the wind. Criticism, condemnation, and complaint are creatures of the wind. They come and go on the wasted breath of lesser beings and have no power over me. The power to control direction belongs to me. Today I will begin to exercise that power. My course has been charted. My destiny is assured.

I have a decided heart. I am passionate about my vision for the future.

I will awaken every morning with an excitement about the new day and its opportunity for growth and change. My thoughts and actions will work in a forward motion, never sliding into the dark forest of doubt or the muddy quicksand of self-pity. I will freely give my vision for the future to others, and as they see the belief in my eyes, they will follow me.

I will lay my head on my pillow at night happily exhausted, knowing that I have done everything within my power to move the mountains in my path. As I sleep, the same dream that dominates my waking hours will be with me in the dark. Yes, I have a dream. It is a great dream, and I will never apologize for it. Neither will I ever let it go, for if I did, my life would be finished. My hopes, my passions, my vision for the future are my very existence. A person without a dream never had a dream come true.

I have a decided heart. I will not wait.

I know that the purpose of analysis is to come to a conclusion. I have tested the angles. I have measured the probabilities. And now I have made a decision with my heart. I am not timid. I will move now and not look back. What I put off until tomorrow, I will put off until the next day as well. I do not procrastinate. All my problems become smaller when I confront them. If I touch a thistle with caution, it will prick me, but if I grasp it boldly, its spines crumble into dust.

I will not wait. I am passionate about my vision for the future. My course has been charted. My destiny is assured.

I have a decided heart.

SEVEN

✛

DAVID FELT THE SWAYING OF THE *SANTA MARIA* AS he looked up from the parchment. Columbus turned to stare as David stood up and saw that he was no longer in the crow's nest, but seemingly had his feet planted firmly in midair, moving at an ever increasing pace away from the ship. Columbus smiled and raised his hand. David did the same and suddenly streaked away so fast that his vision perceived a thousand images of Columbus as the *Santa Maria* stretched out like strobes of light in the tail of a comet.

In the next instant, David was standing in a small room. The air smelled strongly of mildew with just a hint of lye soap. The only light in the room came from a bare bulb hanging on a wire from the ceiling. David quickly counted seven people within several steps. He frowned. Incredibly, they were motionless. A man and a woman were seated at a tiny table. Two teenagers, a boy and a girl, were sprawled on the floor, an interrupted card game between them, and the rest, two men and a woman, appeared to have stopped in midstride. Every person wore a look of terror.

David heard knocking on the wall behind him and the muffled voices of men. As he turned to look, he noticed a small girl he had missed before. She was thin and sharply featured with dark wavy hair and eyes so black that they shined. She appeared to be perhaps twelve or thirteen and wore a faded blue cotton dress that seemed at home in the dingy room.

David understood why he had not seen her at first. She was standing right next to him, so close that he had literally looked over her. This girl, too, David saw, was not moving, but as he caught her gaze, she slowly raised a finger to her lips.

The knocking seemed to run in a pattern, first high on the wall, then to the middle and on toward the floor. The muffled voices would then move to the right, and the knocking would begin again. High, center, low. For almost five full minutes, David remained still as he listened to the sounds on the other side of the wall.

Once, one of the voices began yelling something unintelligible, and they heard several people running. At that point, the woman sitting at the table reached out to hold the man's hand. Both closed their eyes. Except for the small girl putting her finger to her lips, it was the only movement David saw from any of them.

After what seemed an eternity, the knocking ceased. There was no more running, no voices, just the tense silence of the little room. And still, no one moved. For a full minute, then two. Finally, the man at the table took a deep breath and blew it out with a whoosh. "Het is oke nu allemaal," he said quietly. "It is all right now, everyone." And with that, the people in the room shook their heads and softly began talking to each other.

"This was close, I am thinking," said the teenage boy on the floor. "If there had been dogs . . ." He let the thought just hang there, never finishing the sentence.

A tall woman, her hair rolled tightly into a bun, began weeping softly. "Now then, Petronella," her husband said as he put his arms around her. "We are safe. Shhh, hush now." He turned to the boy and said sternly, "Peter, that'll be enough about what might have been. You've upset your mother and most everyone else, I expect. We'll have no more about dogs."

"I was just saying . . . ," Peter began.

"Yes," the man interrupted, "and I was just saying that will be enough!"

David watched as the man led his wife into a narrow room to his left. Before the door closed, he saw a mattress on the floor and a stack of movie-star magazines. The young girl gently moved David to a corner and whispered, "Stay here for now, but when I leave the room, follow me."

She moved toward the couple sitting at the table. The man looked tired, but even though his clothes were worn, he was clean-shaven except for a small mustache. What little hair he had left on his head was neatly combed. David thought him a rather distinguished sort. The woman sitting across from him, her hair in a bun just like the other woman had worn, was ghostly pale, as if she'd recently been ill. Nevertheless, she smiled as the girl approached.

"Papa," the girl said. "May I have your permission to go upstairs?"

The man smiled. "Time to be alone again, is it?"

"Yes, Papa."

"Then certainly you may go," he said. She gave a glance to David and moved resolutely to a stairway at the back of the room. Seeing her reach the stairs, her father spoke once more, his smile fading.

"Anne." She stopped and turned. "Keep away from the window."

"Yes, Papa," she nodded and without a sound moved up the staircase and out of sight.

David followed quickly, careful not to bump any of the people as he passed. Ascending the stairs, he saw the girl motioning for him to hurry. The staircase appeared to go directly into the ceiling, but as David soon saw, there was a hatch cover that provided an entrance to the attic.

As soon as they were inside, the girl replaced the cover

and said, "I am so excited to meet you that I almost cannot breathe!" She clapped her hands together quickly, but softly. "This is thrilling, is it not?"

"Yes," David said, grinning at her enthusiasm. He glanced around. There was not a stick of furniture or a box of anything stored in this attic, just dust and dirt. "I suppose *thrilling* would be a proper choice of words."

"I expected you, did you know?" she said. "A dream is how. I even know your name. It is Mr. Ponder. I wrote you a note just this morning. Should I get it now?"

"No, no." David chuckled. "Slow down just a minute. You have me at a disadvantage. I don't even know where I am!"

"Why, you are in Amsterdam," the child said. She took David's hand and pulled him toward a window. "Come," she said with a little smile, "I will show you the city."

Across the bare attic, there loomed a large nine-paned window. Three of the panes had been separated from the other six by a brick column. The window itself was dirty, almost as brown as the attic. "Is this the window," David asked, "that your father warned you to stay away from?"

"Yes, yes," she said as she nodded her head, "but it is all right to peek from the corner." And with that she got down on her hands and knees and exclaimed impatiently, "You too! Come now!"

David got down on his hands and knees and followed

the girl to the edge of the window where she was waiting underneath the sill. When he reached her, he turned to sit on the floor, his back to the wall. She sat with her legs folded underneath her and leaned her right shoulder to the dirty plaster. As he settled himself into a more comfortable position, David said, "I heard your father call you Anne."

"Yes," she replied. "And my sister's name is Margot. She is very quiet. She was the one playing cards with the boy downstairs. His name is Peter. Peter Van Daan."

"What is your last name?" David asked.

"Frank," she said simply. "My papa's name is Otto, and Edith is my mother. Peter's parents are Mr. Herman and Mrs. Petronella. She was the one who cried, but of course, she always cries. The other man you saw was Dr. Dussel. You did see him, didn't you? He was sitting on the floor near the door to my room, but of course, you don't know which room is mine, so maybe you didn't see him. In any case, he's not a doctor really. He's a dentist . . ."

David wasn't certain how long Anne talked. He was not really listening anyway. His mind was a jumble of thoughts and emotions. *Anne Frank,* he thought. *Anne Frank! This is the young girl whose diary I read in high school.*

". . . so Peter brought him with us," Anne continued, ignoring the stunned look on the face of her guest. "Mouschi is wonderful, though not as loving as my own dear cat, Moortje, who is still at home. Mouschi is black as coal dust. Moortje, on the other hand . . ."

I am in the annex, David thought. The annex, he knew, was a secret location consisting of several rooms connected to the back of a warehouse. Anne and her family were Dutch Jews in hiding during the Nazi occupation of Holland.

". . . don't you think?" Anne said as she looked directly at David, obviously waiting for a response.

David was startled by the pause in her nonstop chatter. He had been so caught up in his surroundings that he hadn't actually been listening. "I'm sorry. What did you say?" he asked uncomfortably.

"I said," Anne answered slowly, "that Peter is very handsome, don't you think?"

"Peter?" David wrinkled his brow. "Oh, the boy downstairs, yes. Yes, he is!"

"I let him kiss me sometimes. On the cheek, of course."

"Of course," David said seriously. "Anne," David began in an effort to change the subject, "how long have you been here?"

"One year and four months," she said quickly.

"Do you know today's date?"

"Certainly. Today is Thursday, October 28, 1943. We went into hiding last year on the first Sunday in July, the fifth it was." Anne glanced up at the window above. "None of us have been outside in a very long time."

"How do you get food in here?"

"Miep."

"Who is . . . ?"

"Miep is Papa's secretary. She still comes to work in the warehouse every day. After hours, she and her husband, Henk, move the bookcase in the accounting room and come through the door behind it."

"Anne," David said. "When I arrived . . ."

"Oh, yes," Anne broke in, "that was so terrifying! You appeared directly in front of me, and I was the only one who could see you! Have you done that before? Does it hurt?"

David smiled in spite of his aggravation at being interrupted. He supposed he could understand her excitement. After all, a new person with whom to talk must be thrilling after sixteen months. "Yes, I have done it before, and no, it doesn't hurt." David reached out to touch her arm as he tried again to ask his question. "Anne, when I arrived, what, or who, was knocking on the walls?"

"Nazi soldiers," Anne said. "Papa calls them Gestapo. He says they dress in black. They have come now two times. We are quiet and they go away." She turned and got up on her knees, rising carefully to put one eye in the corner of the window. "If you do this, you can see most of Amsterdam."

David rose and looked out the opposite corner. To his left, he saw a huge chestnut tree reaching almost one hundred feet into the air and casting its last shade of the day into the attic window. A clock tower stood majestically across the street. Its spires and gables were the centerpiece of the city.

"That's the Westerkerk," Anne said, referring to the clock. "I can lie here and watch the hands move." Anne laid herself out flat on the floor. "Lie down," she said. "See for yourself."

David eased himself down beside the young girl and looked up. There, framed in the window as if by divine providence, was the clock face of the Westerkerk tower. It was, he noticed, almost six o'clock in the evening. David looked at Anne, staring intently at the clock, and thought of his own daughter. She and Anne were about the same age. He tried to imagine Jenny in this situation. What would she do? How would she react? Or, for that matter, how would he?

"What are you thinking?" David asked softly.

"About the clock," Anne said. "Sometimes I wish for it to speed up, and at other times I beg it to slow down. But it never hears me. It is always the same."

David jumped as whistles and loud, angry voices blasted the silence of the street four floors below them. Anne did not move but continued gazing at the clock. "What is going on?" David asked.

"It is a razia," Anne answered with no emotion. "They are rounding up Jews. It makes me wonder about my friends. I don't know what has happened to any of them." For several moments she was quiet, thoughtful. David said nothing. Then she looked directly at him and said, "Everyone is being taken away to camps. Did you know? The Germans say that the Jews are working and living comfortably, but it is not true."

David was careful with his words. "How do you know that?"

Anne shrugged. "We all know," she said. "Letters are censored, of course, but occasionally, the truth is made known. Miep received a postcard from a friend that said the food was good and conditions were superb, but at the end of the message, he wrote: 'Give my regards to Ellen de Groot.'" She paused. "The words were Dutch, of course. The German censors did not know that *ellende* means 'misery.' *Groot* is 'terrible.' His intent was to convey a message of terrible misery."

Without warning, the Westerkerk clock tower began to chime. Six times the clapper hammered out its message of time on the lip of the massive bell. Less than seventy feet away, Anne merely placed her hands over her ears and smiled at David, who had nearly jumped out of his skin when the chiming began.

"It is only a bit too loud," Anne said, giggling at her understatement.

David smiled. "I'm glad you think it's funny," he said. "I

thought my head was about to come off! How do you sleep with that thing ringing day and night?"

"Actually," Anne said, "we don't even notice it much anymore. Mrs. Petronella is the only one of us who even makes comment. Papa says the clock is a good thing for her because it provides something to complain about every hour on the hour!"

David laughed. "What about you?" he asked. "What do you complain about?"

"I do not complain," Anne said. "Papa says complaining is an activity just as jumping rope or listening to the radio is an activity. One may choose to turn on the radio, and one may choose not to turn on the radio. One may choose to complain, and one may choose not to complain. I choose not to complain."

David stared at the sincere little girl for a moment, then said, "I don't mean any offense to what your father has taught you, but have you taken a look around here? These are pretty rough conditions for anyone, never mind a girl your age. How can you *not* complain?"

Anne tilted her head to the side as if she were having difficulty understanding. Sweeping a lock of hair from her eyes, she said patiently, "Our very lives are fashioned by choice, Mr. Ponder. First we make choices. Then our choices make us.

"Rough conditions? Yes, an ungrateful person might see

101

this place as too small for eight people, a diet that is limited and portions that are too meager, or only three dresses for two girls to share. But gratefulness is also a choice. I see an annex that hides eight people while others are being herded onto railway cars. I see food that is generously provided by Miep, whose family uses their ration cards for us. I see an extra dress for my sister and me while there are surely others who have nothing. I choose to be grateful. I choose not to complain."

David was amazed at the self-control that Anne seemed to possess. He tucked one leg under the other, sitting cross-legged, and shook his head as if to clear the cobwebs. "Are you honestly telling me that you are always in a good mood?"

Anne had folded her legs to mimic the way David was sitting. As she draped her dress over her knees, she laughed. "Of course not, silly! But if I ever find myself in a bad mood, I immediately make a choice to be happy. In fact, it is the first choice I make every day. I say out loud to my mirror, 'Today, I will choose to be happy!' I smile into the mirror and laugh even if I am sad. I just say, 'Ha, ha, ha, ha!' And soon, I am happy, exactly as I have chosen to be."

David was now shaking his head in wonder. "You are a very special young lady, Miss Frank."

"Thank you," Anne said. "That is also a choice."

David leaned forward. "Really," he said with his eyebrows raised. "You've got me now. Explain."

"My life—my personality, my habits, even my speech—is a combination of the books I choose to read, the people I choose to listen to, and the thoughts I choose to tolerate in my mind. Before the war, when I was a little girl, my papa took me to Het Vondel Park on a Saturday afternoon to hear the orchestra play. At the end of the concert, from behind the musicians, a hundred helium balloons of red and blue and yellow and green floated up into the sky. It was so exciting!

"I tugged on Papa's arm and asked, 'Papa, which color balloon will go the highest?' And he said to me, 'Anne, it's not the color of the balloon that is important. It's what's inside that makes all the difference.'"

For a moment, Anne was quiet and the attic still. She seemed so deep in thought that David barely breathed. Then she looked David directly in the eye, lifted her chin, and said, "Mr. Ponder, I don't believe that being Jewish or Aryan or African has any bearing on what one can become. Greatness does not care if one is a girl or a boy. If, in fact, it is what's inside us that makes all the difference, then the difference is made when we choose what goes inside."

Anne turned and looked toward the clock again. David had not noticed the darkness that had filled the attic, but now realized that only the glow of the light from the

Westerkerk tower enabled him to see Anne's face. "I must get ready for dinner soon," she said. "Come with me to my room. I have written something for you."

David followed Anne through the hatch in the attic, down the stairs, and back into the living area. "Dinner is almost on the table, dear," her mother said as the two walked by. "Five minutes. No longer."

Anne led David to a door that was situated to the right of the staircase. As they walked inside and closed the door behind them, David could see that the room was no larger than a closet. A small mattress lay on the floor with two stacks of books beside the only pillow. "Margot and I share this room," Anne said. "It is very close, but we respect each other's privacy."

David didn't see how anyone could hope to have any privacy in this tiny room. On the wall at the foot of the bed hung a simple white dress. The hem, sleeves, and neckline were stitched in small red flowers. Above the head of the bed were pictures cut from magazines and newspapers that had been glued to the wall. Pointing to the array, David asked, "Are these yours, or do they belong to your sister?"

"They are mine." Anne smiled. "Beautiful, aren't they?"

David looked more closely. There was a picture of Greta Garbo and one of Ginger Rogers. A picture of the head of the statue of David by Michelangelo was positioned over a picture of a house in the country. To the left was a black-and-white photo of a rose that someone had colored pink and a large picture of chimpanzees having a tea party. Spread all over the wall were pictures of cute, cuddly babies. "Yes, they are beautiful," David said. "What do they represent?"

"My future," Anne whispered softly as she reached out to touch the picture of the rose. "These are the people I want to meet, the places I want to see, and the things I want in my life. Laughter and love and a home with a husband, maybe Peter, and lots of babies." Suddenly, tears came to her eyes.

David reached out, his hand cupping her head and drawing her to him. Anne put her arms around David's neck as he sank to his knees. As Anne sniffled and sobbed, tears also ran down David's cheeks. He felt such deep admiration for this child. Her courage and wisdom were those of a person who had already lived a lifetime. And in a way, he knew, she had.

Anne eased away to dry her eyes on the sleeve of her dress. "I'm sorry," she said. "I didn't mean to make you uncomfortable."

"I wasn't uncomfortable, Anne," David said as he dried his own eyes. "You remind me of my daughter. Her name is Jennifer. We call her Jenny. She is about your age, and I think you and she are the two prettiest girls I have ever seen."

Anne blushed. "Thank you for saying so." She looked back at the wall and reached out to touch the rose picture again. "May I ask you a question?" she said.

"Certainly," David replied.

"If your Jenny were here instead of me, would she be afraid?"

David could feel the pulse pounding in his head. "I think that she probably would be afraid, Anne. Are you?"

Anne pulled her hand down from the rose and clasped both hands in front of her. Momentarily, she cut her eyes toward David, then back to the pictures. "Sometimes," she said. "But most often, I choose not to be. Papa says, 'Fear is a poor chisel with which to carve out tomorrow.'"

Anne turned and faced David. "I will have a tomorrow, Mr. Ponder. Margot and Mrs. Petronella, they make fun of me. They call me a Pollyanna. They say that I live in a dream world, that I do not face reality. This is not true. I know that the war is horrible. I understand that we are in terrible danger here. I do not deny the reality of our situation. I deny the finality of it. This, too, shall pass."

Anne knelt down and reached under the mattress. She pulled out a red-orange checkered clothbound book. "This is my diary," she said. "Papa gave it to me for my birthday, June twelfth." She thumbed through the pages quickly until she found what she was looking for. "These are yours," she said and carefully tore several pages from the small journal.

David took the pages from her hand and watched as she placed what he knew to be her life's work back under the dirty mattress. "Thank you, Anne."

She stood awkwardly in front of him for a long moment. "Will you tell your daughter Jenny that I said hello?"

David smiled. "Yes, I will."

Anne paused again. "I must go eat," she said. "You will be gone when I return?"

"Yes."

"Then remember me," Anne said, smiling. "I will remember you. But most of all, both of us must remember that life itself is a privilege, but to live life to its fullest— well, that is a choice!"

With those words, Anne hugged David and quickly left the room, softly closing the door behind her. David sat down on the mattress and looked up at the pictures on the wall. For several minutes he listened to the quiet murmuring of the Franks and their friends eating dinner. Then he put the pages Anne had given him in his lap. These were words he fully expected to change his life. Four small pages, written with a pencil, in the hand-writing of a little girl.

THE FIFTH DECISION FOR SUCCESS

Today I will choose to be happy.

Beginning this very moment, I am a happy person, for I now truly understand the concept of happiness. Few others before me have been able to grasp the truth of the physical law that enables one to live happily every day. I know now that happiness is not an emotional phantom floating in and out of my life. Happiness is a choice. Happiness is the end result of certain thoughts and activities, which actually bring about a chemical reaction in my body. This reaction results in a euphoria that, while elusive to some, is totally under my control.

Today I will choose to be happy. I will greet each day with laughter.

Within moments of awakening, I will laugh for seven seconds. Even after such a small period of time, excitement has begun to flow through my bloodstream. I feel different. I am different! I am enthusiastic about the day. I am alert to its possibilities. I am happy!

Laughter is an outward expression of enthusiasm, and I know that enthusiasm is the fuel that moves the world. I laugh throughout the day. I laugh while I am alone, and I laugh in conversation with others. People are drawn to me because I have laughter in my heart. The world belongs to the enthusiastic, for people will follow them anywhere!

Today I will choose to be happy. I will smile at every person I meet.

My smile has become my calling card. It is, after all, the most potent weapon I possess. My smile has the strength to forge bonds, break ice, and calm storms. I will use my smile constantly. Because of my smile, the people with whom I come in contact on a daily basis will choose to further my causes and follow my leadership. I will always smile first. That particular display of a good attitude will tell others what I expect in return.

My smile is the key to my emotional makeup. A wise man once said, "I do not sing because I am happy; I am happy because I sing!" When I choose to smile, I become the master of my emotions. Discouragement, despair, frustration, and fear will always wither when confronted by my smile. The power of who I am is displayed when I smile.

Today I will choose to be happy. I am the possessor of a grateful spirit.

In the past, I have found discouragement in particular situations until I compared the condition of my life to others less fortunate. Just as a fresh breeze cleans smoke from the air, so a grateful spirit removes the cloud of despair. It is impossible for the seeds of depression to take root in a thankful heart.

My God has bestowed upon me many gifts, and for these I will remember to be grateful. Too many times I have offered up the prayers of a beggar, always asking for more and forgetting to give thanks. I do not wish to be seen as a greedy child, unappreciative and disrespectful. I am grateful for sight and sound and breath. If ever in my life there is a pouring out of blessings beyond that, then I will be grateful for the miracle of abundance.

I will greet each day with laughter. I will smile at every person I meet. I am the possessor of a grateful spirit.

Today I will choose to be happy.

EIGHT

✦

DAVID FINISHED READING THE WORDS ANNE HAD prepared and wiped at a tear clinging to his chin. Blinking his eyes, he folded the pages, placed them in the tobacco pouch, shoved the pouch into his pocket, and stood up. He reached out to touch the picture of the rose Anne had glued to the wall. With his finger, David traced the stem from the bottom of the photograph to its center. Touching the bloom, he smiled at the waxy feeling of the pink crayon that had been used to color the black-and-white picture.

Slowly, the rose began to distort. The edges appeared fuzzy and the shape of the bloom pulsed. David pulled his hand back and wiped his eyes. With his left elbow and forearm, he steadied himself against the wall. There, for a moment, he was mildly dizzy, but the feeling quickly passed.

Opening his eyes, David examined the picture again. It was still blurry but seemed to be clearing. He squinted and moved his face only inches from the flower. There! Now it was in focus. He saw the petals of the rose so sharply, so distinctly, that it seemed to have depth. Tentatively, without moving his face, David reached out with his right hand and, using just one finger, touched the rose. Startled, David's breath caught in his throat. The rose was real.

For a moment, he froze. Shifting his eyes, David saw that his left arm was now braced against an old desk. Easing himself away from the rose, he noticed that it stood in a simple crystal vase on the edge of the desk. Next to the rose sat a pitcher of water and four glasses. David stood erect and looked around. He was in a room of some sort . . . no, a tent. It was a rather large tent, he noted, made of white canvas, enclosing an area of approximately fifteen by twenty feet. The floor was dead grass, and except for the desk and three plain wooden chairs, the tent was empty.

Hearing activity of some sort, David moved to the closed flap of the tent's entrance. Carefully, he eased the loose canvas door aside several inches. About seventy-five feet away on a raised platform or makeshift stage, a man stood alone behind a podium. He was facing away from the tent, speaking to thousands of people. David saw saddled horses and carriages and wagons interspersed among the throng. Many had parasols to ward off the sun, and they had spread quilts on the ground or sat atop their wagons.

David saw that the tent and the stage were on top of a hill surrounded by large trees. Since most of their leaves had dropped and the temperature was comfortable even in the tent, David supposed he had arrived in this place during October or maybe even November. In any case, it was autumn, he decided, and judging by the sun, it was somewhere close to noon.

Beyond the crowd, David saw fields and broken forest land that stretched as far as he could see from his limited vantage point. The hills and pastures within his view gave David a strange feeling. The area seemed eerily familiar, though he couldn't quite place how or why.

Perhaps, David thought, *the speaker holds the key to why I am here.* Turning his attention once again toward the stage, David observed that the gentleman, from behind, appeared to be elegantly dressed. He wore gray pants over polished black boots, and a high white collar rose from the back of a black coat complete with tails. His flowing gray hair completed a look of distinction.

In addition, the man appeared to be quite the orator. David noted how he paced the stage and gestured dramatically with his hands. His audience certainly seemed enthralled. They had laughed as a group twice during the short time David watched from the doorway of the tent. David couldn't quite hear the speaker's presentation, for there was no microphone or sound system of any kind, and because the man faced away from him, David could catch only a word here and there.

Suddenly, the crowd thundered a loud and sustained applause. David looked closely as the speaker returned to the podium, which was on the speaker's right and slightly behind him at that moment. As the man waited for the ovation to die away, David got a clear view of his features. His hairline receded from a clean-shaven face. The man's eyebrows were bushy; his nose and ears were a bit large for his head. David didn't recognize him at all.

Disappointed and somewhat confused, David eased himself back inside the tent. For several moments he stood there, wondering where he was and who he had been watching on stage. *Is that the person I am here to see?* he asked himself. David moved to a chair beside the desk and sat down heavily. Pouring himself a glass of water, he couldn't shake the uneasy feeling that he was somehow connected to this place.

Just then, above the continuous sound of the speaker, David heard the crowd begin to murmur. For almost half a minute, the audience's talking among themselves easily drowned out the voice of the man on stage. David rose from his chair and quickly walked toward the tent door. Before he reached the entrance, however, he heard the sound of horses' hooves and creaking leather saddles just outside. Hearing voices approach, David stepped to the corner of the tent as one man walked inside.

He was a young man of about twenty-five, impeccably

groomed in a long coat and high collar. His hair was parted crisply in the middle, and his thin mustache ran in a perfect line above his lips. With the presence of a person who is accustomed to being in charge, the young man strode across the tent directly to the desk. He opened each drawer and carefully inspected the contents before closing it.

David saw him pause for the briefest moment when he spied David's glass of water. The young man picked up the glass and frowned. He was obviously quite aggravated. Shaking his head from side to side with little jerks, he took the glass to the far corner of the tent and poured the remainder of the water onto the ground. Curiously, David thought, he then placed the empty glass in his coat pocket and moved back to the desk where he proceeded to examine the remaining glasses and pitcher.

He picked up the pitcher and looked intently into the water. Then he smelled the water. Finally, he poured a small amount into one of the three glasses left on the desk and carefully tasted it. Satisfied, he then placed *that* glass into his other coat pocket, looked cautiously around the tent, and exited.

David took a deep breath. Evidently, that person was not the one he was there to see. The man hadn't even noticed him standing in plain sight. Before David had time to move, the tent flap opened again.

Bending almost double in order to fit through the

door, this man entered with his hat under his arm. As the tent flap closed behind him, the tall man straightened, glanced around, and saw David. He smiled and with two quick strides stood before David, extending his right hand. "Mr. Ponder, isn't it?" the man said with a twinkle in his eye.

David's mouth was open and his knees felt as if they might collapse. He wanted to say, "Yes, sir," or "How do you do?" or "Nice to meet you," or anything, but his throat was so dry that nothing came out. Becoming aware of the bemused expression on the gentleman's face and seeing that his hand was still extended, David did the only appropriate thing. He shook the hand of Abraham Lincoln.

"I . . . I am honored, sir," David managed to stammer.

"The honor is mine, Mr. Ponder," the president replied. "After all, it is you who has traveled the greater distance for this occasion."

Lincoln wore white riding gloves, gauntlets, that contrasted sharply with his totally black attire and made his large hands seem larger still. Removing the gloves, he walked to the desk and, after placing the gloves and his hat on the far side, asked, "Won't you join me please in refreshment?"

Seeing that the president had indicated the pitcher of water, David accepted his offer and asked, "Sir, where are we?"

Lincoln held up one long finger, then poured David a glass of water. Pouring his own glass, he drank it all, poured another, and sat down. "Bring up a chair," he said as he drew his own from behind the desk.

As David sat down, he watched the sixteenth president of the United States cross his legs at the knee and loosen his high starched collar. He was dressed well. His hair was combed, his beard neatly trimmed, and yet he still appeared somewhat . . . well, disheveled. David noticed that the president seemed oversized in all physical respects. His legs, arms, hands, even his face appeared to be too long. David smiled to himself as he realized that Abraham Lincoln looked exactly like every picture he'd ever seen of the man.

David's only surprise, after Lincoln's sudden appearance, was the president's voice. It was not a rich baritone as he had heard it portrayed in numerous movies, but a higher-pitched tenor.

Lincoln placed the glass on the desk and said, "Riding horseback always makes me thirsty, though I'm usually too embarrassed to drink in front of the horse. After all," he chuckled, "I'm not the one who has done the work!" David laughed politely. "So, Mr. Ponder, you wish to know where we are."

"Yes, sir, and please call me David."

"Thank you," Lincoln said as he slightly inclined his

head to the younger man. "David, I am here for two reasons today. First, to dedicate a cemetery. That, by the way, is where we are now . . . Gettysburg, Pennsylvania."

Shivers ran down David's back. "And the date?"

"November nineteenth, eighteen sixty-three."

No wonder this place seems so familiar, David thought. *I was here four months ago. Or was it only an hour?* He shook his head to clear his thoughts. "Mr. President, you mentioned two reasons you came here. What was the second?"

Lincoln smiled. "Why, to meet you, of course." David's eyes widened. "You are certainly more important than any remarks I might share with those in attendance today. This cemetery is about the past. You are about the future!"

David looked away. "I appreciate your confidence," he said, "but I'm not sure it's justified. At the moment, I'm just hoping there is a future. I am actually going through the worst time in my life right now."

"Congratulations are in order then! Better days are most assuredly ahead." The president then raised his water glass and exclaimed, "To us, two men experiencing the worst life has to offer."

David didn't respond. He wasn't sure whether Lincoln was teasing him or not. "I'm not kidding," he said slowly.

"Oh, let me promise you," Lincoln said with a tight smile, "neither am I." He reached to his right, across the desk, and picked up his hat. It was the tall black stovepipe that had become as much a part of the man as any image David could remember. For a time, Lincoln let his fingers play softly across the large silk band. "This is a piece of cloth I carry with me in memory of Willie, my little boy. He died only a few months ago." He took a deep breath and sighed. "Now my son Tad has taken to bed . . . deathly ill. And as you might imagine, Mrs. Lincoln did not agree that I should be here today."

"Why did you come?"

"Duty. And the fact that I knew I could choose to pray for my son while wandering about the White House or pray as I continued in pursuit of the task that has been placed before me. I am quite confident the Almighty hears my cry no matter the location. Surely, His arms stretch from Washington to Gettysburg. I also believe the good Lord would rather me pray and work, not pray and wait."

The president shifted position in the chair and crossed his arms. "You know, I mentioned a moment ago that we were two men who were experiencing the worst life has to offer. That is true in a smaller, selfish way, and I must confess my propensity toward self-serving behavior. Actually, it seems to be one of my life's most constant battles. In a larger sense, however, we are being presented an enormous opportunity for change and the betterment of ourselves."

"The betterment of ourselves? You're talking about what we call 'personal growth.' I'm not sure that I want any more personal growth," David said.

"Of course not!" Lincoln responded. "And wouldn't that be the easy choice to make? In fact, it is the most popular choice on the planet! But the question you are facing at this particular point in your life is: How powerful do you want to be?"

David tilted his head to the side. Confused, he said, "I'm lost here. In the first place, what does personal growth have to do with power? And in the second place, no offense, but I have no interest in power anyway."

Leaning forward, Lincoln said, "Mr. Ponder . . . David, if that is true, if you have no interest in power, then an incalculable amount of attention is being wasted on you. Some of it at this very moment!"

David wasn't certain whether to be insulted or not. He began to speak. "I was not the one who . . ."

Lincoln reached over and touched David's knee. Smiling patiently, but interrupting firmly, he said, "David." As David became silent, the president leaned back in his chair. With his dark eyes still on David and the smile still on his face, he said softly, "Now think with me here. Personal growth leads to power. There is a certain level of personal growth that will provide the skills necessary to feed and clothe one's family. There is another level of personal growth that will furnish influence and wisdom in sufficient quantities to be perceived a leader." Lincoln paused. He looked directly into the younger man's eyes. "But to do great deeds, great power is essential.

"Do not run from power. Gather it as you would the finest fruit. Power in the hands of a good person is like a cool drink of water on a hot summer day. It refreshes everyone with whom it comes in contact.

"You see, some people want just enough power to get by. Then there are other people who will acquire enough power to make things more comfortable for their families, and they'll include other less fortunate souls in their charity if the personal growth part of the equation doesn't become too uncomfortable. But there are a few of us, David, who have latched on to this silly idea that we can change the world. We will develop the power to ignore what is popular and do what is right. One person can attain the power to lead hundreds of thousands of people to the promised land of their dreams.

"As children, we were afraid of the dark. Now as adults, we are afraid of the light. We are afraid to step out. We are afraid to become more. But how can we lead others to a destination we have not reached? Keep searching, son. I am urging you to seek the light that to you seems so far in the distance. It will be worth the journey. You will become a lighthouse of personal growth and power, and by your example and leadership, you will prevent many a worthy man from crashing his life upon the rocks of mediocrity."

"Now I see what you're saying," David said, nodding. "So how do I engineer my personal growth? What is important in this . . . this quest?"

"Well," Lincoln began, "it has always been enlightening for me to question myself."

"About what?"

"About myself."

"You question yourself about yourself?"

"Yes," the president said with a laugh. "At least I generally know all the answers!" Stroking his beard with the back of his hand, he continued, "Seriously, questions such as, 'How do other people see me?' and 'What don't they like?' can be quite revealing if answered honestly. When you become a person whom others want to be around, you will have become a person of influence."

"Then I am to work at pleasing people?" David asked.

"Not necessarily. I am speaking primarily of honing the rough edges you might find in your physical appearance and actions such as manners and speech. Of course, I continue to find fertile ground for change in my attitude.

"But you will never please everyone, nor should pleasing everyone be your goal. For example, to seek the approval of someone who is lazy or jealous is to cast your pearls before swine. You will find that God rarely uses a person whose main concern is what others are thinking."

"Are you ever bothered by what other people say about you?" David asked.

The president quickly leaned forward with a serious look on his face. "Why?" he said. "What are they saying?"

Seeing David's shocked expression, Lincoln laughed loudly. "David, I inherited a nightmare from President Buchanan. By the time I was sworn in, seven states had already seceded from the Union, and Jefferson Davis was named president of the Confederate States of America. Just between us, Buchanan was no great help. He left Washington proclaiming himself the last president of the United States.

"As you may know, I am the first ever Republican president. I was elected by a minority of the popular vote, and even some members of my own cabinet view me as third-rate. To many of the elite in Washington, I will always be a country lawyer, a gawky, unrefined out-sider. If I were to concern myself with the newspaper columns that label me dishonest or stupid, if I had my feelings destroyed every time a political opponent called me an ape or a buffoon, I would never be about the work for which I was born!"

Lincoln stood and shoved his hands into his pockets. "Sooner or later, every man of character will have that character questioned. Every man of honor and courage will be faced with unjust criticism, but never forget that unjust criticism has no impact whatsoever upon the truth. And the only sure way to avoid criticism is to do nothing and be nothing!"

As he paused for a breath, Lincoln's attention was diverted by loud, rolling applause from the gathering outside the tent. He grinned and motioned for David to come with him. "Let's see where we are in the program."

Moving to the tent's entrance, the president eased the door flap aside, affording them a clear view of the stage. The same gentleman David had seen earlier was still speaking. "Who is he?" David asked quietly.

Without turning, Lincoln answered, "That is our principal orator at this occasion. The Honorable Edward Everett. He was the president of Harvard University and secretary of state under President Fillmore. He can certainly hold an audience in the palm of his hand. Look at the faces of the people. They are transfixed."

"I am sure they are waiting for you, sir," David replied.

Lincoln smiled and carefully dropped the flap. Backing away from the entrance, he said, "I appreciate the compliment, but today I have only a few remarks. I am here for the dedication. I was invited only three weeks ago."

At that instant, the door flap was thrown aside, and the young, smartly dressed man who had been in the tent earlier entered. Lincoln gestured toward him with his hand and said, "John Hay, my personal secretary."

David froze momentarily and then held his laughter as the young man hesitated. He watched as Hay looked from side to side, then glanced around the tent and said hesitantly, "Sir?"

Recovering quickly, Lincoln asked, "How may I be of assistance, John?"

Hay wrinkled his brow, obviously puzzled, and continued to peer cautiously behind the president.

"John," Lincoln said again, snapping Hay to attention, "how may I be of assistance?"

"I . . . ahh . . . excuse the interruption, Mr. President." Now Lincoln stifled a chuckle. David had his hand over his mouth. "Well . . . sir," Hay stammered. "I wanted you to know that when Mr. Everett has concluded, the Baltimore Glee Club will sing an ode written for this occasion. The music will provide the time necessary to escort you from here to the stage."

"Thank you, John," Lincoln said as he moved to the doorway. "The beginning of the music, then, will be my cue to join you outside the tent. Until that time, sir, I trust you will maintain my privacy."

The president pulled back the door flap, an obvious gesture intended to hasten his secretary's departure. Hay ducked through the opening and turned around. Bent over, half inside and half outside the tent, Hay carefully worded his question. "Sir, excuse me, but are you saying that I should not come back inside?"

"That is correct, John."

"So, you will meet me outside the tent when you are ready to go to the stage?"

"Yes, John."

Briefly, Hay paused. Then, still doubled over in the doorway, he said, "Sir, if I may be so bold as to ask—"

"John," Lincoln interrupted.

"Yes, sir?"

"I will meet you outside the tent when I am ready to go to the stage."

"Yes, sir," Hay said resignedly and slid outside the door.

The president closed the canvas and, urging David to follow with a jerk of his head, walked quickly to the desk. As he sat down, tears were streaming down his face as he finally let his laughter burst forth. For several moments, they both laughed heartily.

Gaining control, Lincoln took a deep breath and sighed. "That was extremely close, my friend. Momentarily, I forgot that he could not see you. John is a fine young man. I hate to laugh at his expense, but if the Almighty will forgive me, the look on his face was priceless!"

David chuckled as he sat down, tipping the chair back on two legs into a more comfortable position. "Before your secretary entered, you were talking about your part in this ceremony today."

"Yes." Lincoln's smile disappeared as he cleared his throat. "Yes, today we take pause from our battles to dedicate one ugly reality of this war: a cemetery. There are quite a few of them around now, as you must know. Certainly more than I can dedicate."

Lincoln frowned and continued, "There were more than fifty thousand casualties here. They say blood and gore ran in rivulets on the ground." He was quiet for a moment, and then brightening, he said, "I have Grant now. This will not last much longer."

"Are you winning the war?" David asked.

"We weren't, I can tell you that! But after this battle, Gettysburg, last July, the outcome seems much brighter indeed."

David suddenly had a thought and asked, "Mr. President, are you familiar with an officer in your army by the name of Colonel Joshua Chamberlain? He is with the Twentieth Maine."

Lincoln cocked his head and thought briefly, then said slowly, "No, I don't believe so. Should I know this man?"

"Maybe. He fought here at Gettysburg. When you return to Washington, you might look him up." The president nodded. "I have another question," David continued, "do you believe that God is on your side?"

Lincoln looked at David thoughtfully. "On September twenty-second of last year, I signed a proclamation of emancipation for all slaves specifying that they will be henceforward and forever free. The timing of that gesture is still the subject of some debate. One of my cabinet members made it known to anyone who would listen that a vast majority of the public stood against me and my intention to sign the Emancipation Proclamation. My platform, however, is that while public opinion might sway back and forth, right and wrong do not.

"If we familiarize ourselves with the chains of bondage, we prepare our own limbs to wear them. The spirit of our government and our institutions must be to elevate people, and I am opposed to whatever degrades them. I am of the opinion that right makes might. Therefore, I signed the document, and now we will enforce its effectiveness.

"So your question was, 'Do I believe that God is on our side?' To be quite honest, I haven't given that question very much attention. I am much more concerned with whether we are on God's side."

David remembered something Lincoln had said earlier. "You mentioned Grant," he prompted. "Why will he make such a difference?"

"Because he cares as I do!" came the sharp reply. "It has taken me almost three years to find a general officer whom I don't have to watch over like a nursemaid.

Winfield Scott was my first general in chief. Then McDowell, followed by Fremont, then the disastrous McClellan. Can you imagine? In McClellan, I had a commander of the entire Union army who refused to engage the enemy!

"After McClellan, I appointed Henry Halleck. Halleck is a graduate of West Point and has even written a book on military tactics. I read it last year before his appointment. Fine book, good theory, but books don't fight wars. The man evaded all personal responsibility, lost what little composure he brought to the task, and became nothing more than a first-rate clerk.

"McClernand was next, and all he did was complain about the other generals. It was the odd week I didn't receive a long, rambling communication critical of something Sherman or Grant had done. After McClernand, I suffered through Rosecrans, then Burnside, and finally Nathaniel P. Banks.

"Naturally, the day I announced my intentions to promote General Grant, I was vilified in the press. Actually, many people have been pushing for Grant's dismissal, but I can't spare this man. He fights! I've heard it said that he drinks too much. Well, if I can find out exactly what he's drinking, I'll send a few cases to the other generals!"

David laughed at that comment. Lincoln smiled and continued, "I suppose the point of all this is that Ulysses S.

Grant wants to win as badly as I do. If you are determined to win, you will have to surround yourself with winners. Don't be discouraged by the people you might choose for your team who talk big but produce little. Grant is my tenth try. I just keep putting them in the boat to see who wants to paddle as hard as I do."

"What will you do if . . . when you win?" David asked.

"Do you mean, where will I lead this nation?"

"Yes. After the war, what will be your first priority?"

"That is rather an easy question to answer. In fact, I have spent many hours in prayerful consideration of my response. The first morning after all hostilities cease, I will greet the day with a forgiving spirit."

David was stunned. "How can you? I do not understand!"

"It's a very simple concept actually, and it is the single most important action I take on a regular basis. Forgiveness allows me to be an effective husband, father, friend, and leader of this country."

Confused, David asked, "What does forgiveness have to do with being effective?"

Lincoln thought for a moment, crossed his legs, and answered. "Have you ever been so angry or upset with someone that all you could think of was that person and the horrible way you'd been treated? You think about him when you should be sleeping, and all the things you should have said or would like to say come to mind. When you could be enjoying an evening with your family, your children aren't foremost in your thoughts. That person who offended you is receiving all your energy. You feel as if you might explode." Leaning forward, he asked, "Have you ever felt this way?"

"Yes." David nodded. "I have."

Lincoln relaxed back in his chair and uncrossed his legs. "Well, so have I. I owe business failures, marital strife, and defeats in several political races to those very feelings. But I also owe a great deal of the success I enjoy to the discovery of this simple secret."

"What secret?" David asked.

"The secret of forgiveness," Lincoln responded. "It is a secret that is hidden in plain sight. It costs nothing and is worth millions. It is available to everyone and used by few. If you harness the power of forgiveness, you will be revered, sought after, and wealthy. And not coincidentally, you will also be forgiven by others!"

David looked puzzled. "Just who is it that I am supposed to forgive?"

"Everyone."

"But what if they don't ask for forgiveness?"

Lincoln raised his dark eyebrows and smiled. "Most will not! Amazingly, many of these dastardly people who dare to occupy our minds with angry thoughts are actually wandering about in life without any knowledge of our feelings or any conviction that they have done anything wrong!"

David frowned. "I'm sure that's all true, but I still don't understand how you can forgive someone who doesn't ask for forgiveness!"

"You know," Lincoln began, "for many years, I thought forgiveness was akin to a knighthood—something I bestowed upon some poor wretch who groveled at my feet and begged my blessings. But as I matured and observed successful people, I gained a new perspective on forgiveness.

"I cannot recall a single book, including the Holy Bible, that says in order for you to forgive someone, he or she has to ask for it. Think about this concept! Where is the rule written that before I forgive people, they have to deserve it? Where is it written that to be forgiven by me, you must have wronged me no more than three times? Or seven? Or seventeen?

"The unmistakable truth about forgiveness is that it is not a reward that must be earned; forgiveness is a gift to be given. When I give forgiveness, I free my own spirit to release the anger and hatred harbored in my heart. By granting forgiveness, I free my spirit to pursue my future happily and unencumbered by the anchors of my past. And forgiveness, when granted to others, becomes a gift to myself."

David nodded slowly. "I guess I never considered forgiveness to be something under my control."

Just then, cheers and a long, sustained ovation began outside. The president pulled a pocket watch from his vest and said, "I expect that will be the end of Mr. Everett. Well, not much longer now."

David stood up.

"Sit back down for a moment, son," Lincoln commanded gently. David did so.

"David, you are at a critical point in your life's race, and there exists a person to whom your forgiveness has been withheld for far too long. By the limited authority I have been granted as your host for this short time, I must now warn you that without a forgiving spirit, your effectiveness as a husband, a father, and a leader of people will be at an end. The key to everything your future holds, the touchstone that will, for you, bring dreams into reality, is forgiveness."

David's mouth was open, and a look of confusion and faint astonishment was written in his eyes. "Who is it?" he said. Lincoln merely looked at him. "Sir? Who is it?"

Lincoln stood up and brushed off the front of his jacket and pants. David stood up and said, "Mr. President, you have to tell me who it is!" Lincoln picked up the glass of water and drained the contents. He stepped toward the door, and David put his hand on Lincoln's arm. "Listen!" David said. "You're about to go out there, and I'll never see you again. You as much as said my life would be over if I did not forgive this person. So if it's that important, tell me! Who must I forgive?"

The president looked carefully into David's eyes and said simply, "Yourself."

Tears formed in David's eyes, and he shook his head. Softly, he said, "I didn't think . . ."

"David," Lincoln said as he placed his hands on the younger man's shoulders, "your wife is not mad at you. Your child is not mad at you. Your friends, of which I am one, are not mad at you, and God is not mad at you. So, David . . . ," Lincoln stopped briefly and said with a smile, "don't *you* be mad at you. Forgive yourself. Begin anew."

"Thank you," David said as he wiped his eyes on his shirt-sleeve.

"I am honored to have been of assistance," Lincoln said. Picking up his hat from the desk, he asked, "Would you care to follow me out? You could join the crowd and listen if you wish."

"That would be great," David said. "Thanks! By the way, I'm sorry I took up all your preparation time here in the tent."

"No problem at all," the president responded. "I've been ready with these remarks for about two weeks."

"Really? You know, that's fascinating. When people study you now, or . . . ahh, in the future, one of the things we were all taught is that you wrote this particular speech on the train into Gettysburg."

Lincoln smiled. "No, I wrote the dedication for today back in Washington. I suppose the situation could have been easily confused because I was writing on the train into Gettysburg. In fact . . . ," Lincoln took a piece of paper from the inside band of his stovepipe hat and presented it to David, "I was writing this for you."

David smiled and followed Lincoln to the door. The choir was singing a hymn, and inside the tent, the two men could hear the sounds of twenty thousand people shifting and stretching. Lincoln ducked to go through the door and then, suddenly, he stopped. Turning and straightening to face David, he had a quizzical expression on his face. "You say people study me in the future?"

"Yes, sir," David answered.

Lincoln lowered his voice and narrowed his eyes. "Just between you and me, we *do* win this war, correct?"

"Yes, sir."

With a sly smile on his face and one raised eyebrow, he added one last question. "Grant?"

David grinned. "Yes, sir," he said and followed the great man from the tent.

Outside, David fell back as John Hay and several soldiers immediately surrounded the president and whisked him toward the stage. Lincoln shook hands with Edward Everett, who had remained nearby to hear the president. The choir had finished and left the stage when an emcee, dressed in a fine black tuxedo, approached the podium and sang out, "Ladies and gentlemen, the president of the United States of America, Abraham Lincoln."

With that announcement, twenty thousand people rose to their feet and cheered. David squeezed around to the front of the stage and stood with everyone else. As the applause died, they remained standing. David was just to the right and under his friend when, in a high-pitched, almost shrill voice, Abraham Lincoln spoke the words that would begin the healing of a broken nation:

"Four score and seven years ago, our fathers brought forth upon this continent a new nation, conceived in liberty, and dedicated to the proposition that all men are created equal.

"Now we are engaged in a great civil war, testing whether that nation—or any nation so conceived and so dedicated—can long endure. We are met on a great battlefield of that war. We are met to dedicate a portion of it as the final resting place of those who here gave their lives that that nation might live. It is altogether fitting and proper that we should do this.

"But in a larger sense we cannot dedicate, we cannot consecrate, we cannot hallow this ground. The brave men, living and dead, who struggled here, have consecrated it far beyond our power to add or detract. The world will little note nor long remember what we say here, but it can never forget what they did here. It is for us, the living, rather to be dedicated here to the unfinished work that they have thus far so nobly carried on. It is rather for us to be here dedicated to the great task remaining before us— that from these honored dead we take increased devotion to the cause for which they here gave the last full measure of devotion—that we here highly resolve that the dead shall not have died in vain, that the nation shall, under God, have a new birth of freedom and that the government of the people, by the people, and for the people, shall not perish from the earth."

For a moment, the crowd stood silent. Then all around him, David heard people begin to applaud. Joining them enthusiastically, he watched as Lincoln nodded to the crowd, acknowledging their appreciation, and then waved to the people farthest from the stage. Looking below him, he caught David's gaze and smiled. He then waved to the audience once more, turned, and was gone.

David picked his way through the people and walked to a large beech tree standing alone on the gentle slope of a hill. He was away from the thousands of people as he sat down in the shade of the tree. Hearing the voices of the choir as they sang another hymn from the stage, David unfolded the paper given to him by the sixteenth president of the United States and read.

The Sixth Decision for Success

I will greet this day with a forgiving spirit.

For too long, every ounce of forgiveness I owned was locked away, hidden from view, waiting for me to bestow its precious presence upon some worthy person. Alas, I found most people to be singularly unworthy of my valuable forgiveness, and since they never asked for any, I kept it all for myself. Now, the forgiveness that I hoarded has sprouted inside my heart like a crippled seed yielding bitter fruit.

No more! At this moment, my life has taken on new hope and assurance. Of all the world's population, I am one of the few possessors of the secret to dissipating anger and resentment. I now understand that forgiveness has value only when it is given away. By the simple act of granting forgiveness, I release the demons of the past about which I can do nothing, and I create in myself a new heart, a new beginning.

I will greet this day with a forgiving spirit. I will forgive even those who do not ask for forgiveness.

Many are the times when I have seethed in anger at a word or deed thrown into my life by an unthinking or uncaring person. I have wasted valuable hours imagining revenge or confrontation. Now I see the truth revealed about this psychological rock inside my shoe. The rage I nurture is often one-sided, for my offender seldom gives thought to his offense!

I will now and forevermore silently offer my forgiveness even to those who do not see that they need it. By the act of forgiving, I am no longer consumed by unproductive thoughts. I give up my bitterness. I am content in my soul and effective again with my fellowman.

I will greet this day with a forgiving spirit. I will forgive those who criticize me unjustly.

Knowing that slavery in any form is wrong, I also know that the person who lives a life according to the opinion of others is a slave. I am not a slave. I have chosen my counsel. I know the difference between right and wrong. I know what is best for the future of my family, and neither misguided opinion nor unjust criticism will alter my course.

Those who are critical of my goals and dreams simply do not understand the higher purpose to which I have been called. Therefore, their scorn does not affect my attitude or action. I forgive their lack of vision, and I forge ahead. I now know that criticism is part of the price paid for leaping past mediocrity.

I will greet this day with a forgiving spirit. I will forgive myself.

For many years, my greatest enemy has been myself. Every mistake, every miscalculation, every stumble I made has been replayed again and again in my mind. Every broken promise, every day wasted, every goal not reached has compounded the disgust I feel for the lack of achievement in my life. My dismay has developed a paralyzing grip. When I disappoint myself, I respond with inaction and become more disappointed.

I realize today that it is impossible to fight an enemy living in my head. By forgiving myself, I erase the doubts, fears, and frustration that have kept my past in the present. From this day forward, my history will cease to control my destiny. I have forgiven myself. My life has just begun.

I will forgive even those who do not ask for forgiveness. I will forgive those who criticize me unjustly. I will forgive myself.

I will greet this day with a forgiving spirit.

NINE

✛

DAVID DUG THE TOBACCO POUCH OUT OF HIS pocket. Carefully, he folded the paper and placed it inside the worn canvas. His hand brushed the smooth skin on which King Solomon had written the Second Decision. "One, two, three, four, five, six." David counted the precious pages aloud. *I'm supposed to receive seven,* he thought. *Where will I go next?*

David was tense. Waiting for the experience of leaping across time and space had left him nervous and exhausted. As he looked across the field, he saw Lincoln's party leaving the cemetery on horseback. The president, with his white gauntlets and tall black hat shining in the sunlight, cut a dashing figure. David smiled and shook his head in wonder.

Feelings of weariness overcame David. Unable to keep his eyes open, he put the pouch back in his pocket and lay down. He tried to stay awake and was scared to fall asleep, but he couldn't fight it. Visions of Ellen and Jenny swept over him. "Where are you, Daddy?" Jenny cried. "Come home!" It was a dream, David knew, but he couldn't wake up. He tried to touch them, but they were just out of his reach. *This is crazy,* David thought. *I'm having a dream in the middle of a dream. I have to wake up!*

Ellen stood with her hands on her sobbing daughter's shoulders, comforting the child. "David, we need you," she said.

Wake up! David screamed at himself.

"I'm expecting great things from you, son." It was a man's voice. David swung around to see his father-in-law. There were tears in his eyes. "You promised me you'd take care of my daughter."

David woke up drenched in sweat. He was nauseated but terrified of closing his eyes again. "Too real," he mumbled to himself as he sat up. "That was too real." Disoriented, David saw that he was on a concrete floor surrounded by . . . paper?

Sitting up straight, he rubbed his eyes as his senses cleared. Directly in front of him was more paper. David rolled to his knees and got to his feet. He saw that these were not ordinary pieces of white paper but photographs. And every photograph was of a child. There were banded stacks of photographs placed neatly on shelf after shelf after shelf. Three big baskets holding hundreds of loose photographs stood at the bottom of one row as if waiting to be filed. These were pictures of children of all ages and colors. There were two children in some photographs and just one in many more. David saw others had three children or four, and a few held five or six.

David stepped into an opening on his left. It was an aisle of some sort, and just beyond it stood massive racks of clothing. Walking tentatively, David approached the brightly colored materials and ran his hand over a small coat. Picking up the sleeve of another garment, he recognized it as a coat as well. In fact, he determined quickly that every single article of clothing was a coat. Large ones, small ones, coats and jackets, each on its own individual hanger. "Thousands," David murmured, "maybe hundreds of thousands."

David turned back toward the photographs and gasped. Standing across the aisle gave him a peripheral view of where he had awakened moments before. Close to the pictures, he had not been able to see just how high the shelves were stacked, but looking up, he could not even see a ceiling. There were shelves of photographs one on top of another stacked literally out of sight.

There were no light fixtures in this place, or any lights for that matter, and yet, somehow, everything was bathed in a soft, even glow. To his right, the aisle continued seemingly without end. To his left, the same. There seemed to be no definite structure to the building if it was, in fact, a building. *Am I still dreaming?* David wondered.

Noticing something different on the shelves just past the photographs, David walked slowly down the aisle almost a hundred yards until he saw wheelchairs. Thousands of wheelchairs. Lined up and on shelves. Row after row of nickel-plated, gleaming wheelchairs. Just beyond the wheelchairs were beds—double, single, king, and queen. Then bicycles—all kinds, all colors.

Across from the bicycles were legal documents of some kind. David looked closer. They were automobile titles. The papers, on shelves and bundled as the pictures had been, were spread over an area as large as ten houses and, like everything else in this place, were piled higher than he could see.

Next to the car titles were shoes of every description, each pair in its own separate cubicle. Baby shoes took up a cabinet that David guessed might be sixty or seventy yards long and who knew how high. The baby shoes were followed by cabinets filled with men's and women's dress shoes, galoshes, and sneakers. Hundreds of thousands, maybe millions of shoes, David wasn't sure.

David was sure, however, that he had never been anywhere like this before. The temperature seemed perfect. There was no music, no smell. He had seen no support pilings of any kind or walls or people. *Where am I?* he thought. *What is this place, and what's with this stuff?*

He continued to walk and found new aisles, but none

with an end. He saw blue jeans and medicine and pictures of homes. There were heaters and marriage licenses, roofing shingles and food. Slowly, he worked his way back toward the pictures of the children.

On the way, he passed an area stacked with money. Cash in every currency and denomination. David put his hands on his hips, pursed his lips, and expelled all the air from his lungs. "This makes absolutely no sense at all," he said aloud. Continuing, he counted two hundred and nine steps before the money was no longer beside him.

Soon, David was back where he had begun, even though he knew he had not seen nearly everything. As he turned in a complete circle, gazing all around him, a picture fluttered down from somewhere above. It landed on the floor not far from where David stood. Picking it up, he moved to place it back on a shelf but stopped. Something troubled him about the photograph.

It was a color picture of two children, a boy and a girl each around six or seven years old. They were quite obviously brother and sister, but they looked remarkably similar to Jenny, his own daughter. Their eyes were blue like Jenny's—and Ellen's—and the blond hair lifted into the same cowlick on the front left side.

David shook his head in wonder. He couldn't take his eyes off the photo.

Faintly, almost in a part of his subconscious, David

heard something. Glancing up sharply, he looked down the aisle where he had just been and saw a figure walking toward him. The person was moving from several hundred yards away, steadily and easily. As he approached the area that held the beds and bicycles, David could see that it was a man. He was huge. David was two inches over six feet but saw that this man would tower over him.

David eased a couple of feet to his left, feeling somewhat safer close to the stacks of pictures. He saw that the man had blond, almost golden, curly hair. It was relatively short, touching his eyebrows and just brushing his ears. He wore a robe draped over his shoulders and hanging to his knees. It was white, or maybe light. In fact, this man, who was now no more than fifty feet away, seemed to be dressed in what David could only describe as shades of light.

The man smiled a greeting as he came closer, then stopped and turned to straighten a wheelchair on his right. When he did, David's mouth dropped open. The man had wings.

They were of the purest white and lay close to his shoulder blades. As the man bent to move the wheelchair, David could see that they ran the length of his body, the tips extending almost to the floor. As he stood again to full height, the wings folded in close to his back.

Closing the distance quickly between them, the man stopped and said, "Hello, David Ponder. I am Gabriel."

He was as tall as David had at first thought and built like a warrior. Heavily muscled, yet somehow gentle, he was not threatening in any way. His nose was long and straight, his lips full, and the skin on his face was smooth and devoid of whiskers. But his eyes held David's attention. They were the brightest blue he had ever seen and appeared to have been dusted with flakes of gold.

David's mouth hung open. "You're an angel," he finally managed to say.

"An archangel actually." Gabriel smiled, revealing perfectly even, white teeth. "There is a difference, you know."

"I'm sorry, I . . . ahh . . . I really didn't," David stammered. "Know, I mean. That there was a difference."

"No matter, David Ponder," Gabriel responded. "I am honored to make your acquaintance."

Indicating the photograph David still held in his hand, he said, "May I?"

"Oh . . . sure!" David said and gave it to him.

Gabriel looked at the picture for a moment, then showed it again to David. "Beautiful children, aren't they?" David nodded in agreement and watched as Gabriel placed it in the basket of loose photos.

"So I *am* dead?" David blurted out.

Gabriel wrinkled his forehead and appeared confused. "Excuse me?"

"If I'm with you, then I must be in heaven. And if I'm in heaven, I must be dead."

Gabriel laughed. "No, you are not dead. This is merely a brief stopover, perhaps the most important stopover, in your travel. This is the only destination all travelers have in common."

"Have there been many travelers?" David asked.

"Relatively few," Gabriel said, "when one considers the beginning of time as you know it and the numbers of people with whom we have dealt. But for those who are chosen to travel, an understanding of their true mission begins here, in this place. Joan of Arc, George Washington, and Martin Luther King Jr. all took a step toward destiny from where you now stand."

"Which is where exactly?" David motioned with his hands. "What is this place?"

Gabriel held up one finger. "Not quite yet," he said. "First, let us walk together."

Moving slowly away from the direction in which he had come, Gabriel led David past ceiling fans and air-conditioners, tires and blankets, watches and pictures of animals. Just as there had been photographs of children,

David saw rows and files and stacks of dog pictures, cat pictures, horses, hamsters, birds, turtles, fish, and a few animals he didn't even recognize.

Approaching a vast area stacked neatly with monstrous rolls of carpet, Gabriel stopped, turned, and without warning, asked, "Do you consider yourself a man of faith, David Ponder?"

David frowned. Momentarily thrown, he said, "I'm not sure what you mean."

Gabriel's eyebrows rose. "A simple question actually. Do you consider yourself a man of faith? Does faith guide your everyday actions and emotions? All men are driven by faith or fear—one or the other—for both are the same. Faith or fear is the expectation of an event that hasn't come to pass or the belief in something that cannot be seen or touched. A man of fear lives always on the edge of insanity. A man of faith lives in perpetual reward."

"Reward?" David said, puzzled.

Walking again, Gabriel replied, "Faith is to believe what one has not seen. The reward of faith is to see what one has believed. Do you consider yourself a man of faith, David Ponder?"

"To be honest," David replied, "I have always thought of myself as a man of reason."

Gabriel turned right, leading his guest down a wide

aisle. "Reason never makes room for miracles; faith releases miracles. And in final comparison, faith is a sounder guide than reason. Reason can only be stretched so far, but faith has no limits. The only limit to your realization of tomorrow is the doubt to which you hold fast today."

"Is it realistic for me to work and live, expecting miracles?" David asked.

Gabriel laughed. "You are quite amusing, David Ponder," he said. "What is this word *realistic?* It is never used here."

David stopped. "You *are* kidding, right?"

"Yes," Gabriel said, still smiling, "I am. But it is a fact that great leaders—great achievers—are rarely realistic by other people's standards. Somehow, these successful people, often considered strange, pick their way through life ignoring or not hearing negative expectations and emotions. Consequently, they accomplish one great thing after another, never having heard what cannot be done. That is precisely why one should never tell a young person that something cannot be done. God may have been waiting centuries for someone ignorant enough of the impossible to do that very thing!"

David's attention was momentarily diverted from Gabriel. As they walked, they passed more and more aisles of bricks, rice, computers, rocking chairs, and vast amounts of items that, as far as David could tell, had no connection.

But here was something new, an area of about one hundred feet square with a single, small pedestal standing in the middle. On the pedestal, David saw as he moved closer, was a stack of papers not even a quarter of an inch high.

It had been the light that caught David's attention. The pedestal, removed from any other item in this place, also stood in stark contrast to the soft glow that seemed to permeate every other row or shelf. A bright light focused sharply on the pedestal's papers. As David moved slowly across the empty space, he looked up and around for the light's source. "Hey, where is the light coming from?" he asked. Gabriel only smiled. Seeing he would receive no answer, David moved closer. "May I touch this?"

"Certainly," Gabriel responded.

There were forty to fifty sheets of paper, some of them obviously newer, some yellowed with age. The first was a complicated mathematical equation, as was the second. The third and several other pages showed multidimensional blueprints for different machines of some sort. Scanning quickly, David saw pages of chemical equations, some that almost appeared to be recipes, and one sheet of paper, yellow and wrinkled, that held only one word in the middle. From biology classes years before, David recognized the word as a Latin name for some sort of plant.

Holding the papers in his left hand, David turned to Gabriel and said, "I don't get it. What are these?"

"One of them," Gabriel said as he moved toward David, "I believe it was the eighth page you looked at, is the cure for pancreatic, liver, or colon cancer."

David stared at Gabriel. His hand, still holding the stack of papers, remained partially extended. "What?" he said.

"Yes," Gabriel continued, "also included there is a machine that will regenerate the optic nerve, allowing even those who are blind from birth to see. A variation of that same device is blueprinted on the following page. It regenerates spinal tissue. You are holding cures and vaccinations for muscular dystrophy, cerebral palsy, and believe it or not, the common cold. Page twenty-six is the answer to Sudden Infant Death Syndrome, and page fourteen, you might be interested to know, is a liquid formula to be swabbed at the back of a child's throat. It painlessly shrinks and removes tonsils in less than six hours."

David was stunned. Barely able to comprehend Gabriel's explanation, he slowly thumbed through the papers again. "But I don't . . . ," he started and stopped. "Am I supposed to take these?"

"No," Gabriel said.

Flushing with anger and confusion, David sputtered, "Then what is the purpose? I mean, why . . . ?" He couldn't find the words. Tears of exhaustion sprang to his eyes. Embarrassed and overwhelmed, David placed the papers on the pedestal and ignored the crack in his voice as he said too loudly, "What is going on? All these things . . . these cures . . . my daughter needs her tonsils taken out. Did you know that?"

"Yes."

For several seconds, David stared open-mouthed at the angel. Then the corners of his mouth sagged and tears streamed down his face as he tried desperately to regain some sense of comprehension. Finally, David yelled, "Do you know I can't afford the operation?"

"Yes."

The frustration of a lifetime seemed to well out of David's soul at that very moment. An agonized cry escaped his throat as he sank to a squatting position. With his left arm on his knee and his right fist ground into the floor, David balanced there and cried bitterly. He cried for Ellen and Jenny. He missed them. Would he ever see them again? Did he deserve to see them again? He cried for the people he had let down in his life—his parents, his friends, his coworkers—and he cried for himself.

After a few minutes had passed, David eased into a sitting position on the floor and sat with his knees bunched under his chin. Calmer now, he tried to catch his breath and wiped his face on the sleeve of his shirt.

Gabriel had not moved. His face was not devoid of compassion, but he offered no physical comfort or suggestion of great sympathy.

David turned his face up to the angel and asked, "Why am I here?" Gabriel held out a hand to help David to his feet. Taking it, David stood and straightened his pants.

Gabriel smiled. "Why do you think you're here?"

"I don't know," David said as he sniffed loudly.

"Then it is not time for you to know," Gabriel said. "Come."

They continued their walk past the pedestal. David took one last look at it as they moved out of sight. Instantly, he again noticed the incredible quantities of an endless variety of items. Some were ordinary. There were electrical cables and light bulbs. Some were not so ordinary. "What is this?" David asked, pointing to a piece of machinery as they passed.

"That bit of equipment," Gabriel responded, "renders any moveable object collision-proof. The design is a combination of laser and sound-wave technology effective on anything from automobiles to a jumbo jet."

David ran his fingers through his hair. "If you won't tell me what this place is and you won't say why I am here, then let me ask you a different question." Gabriel nodded. "Why are all these things here?"

Brushing his hand over one of the many vacuum cleaners they were walking by, Gabriel appeared deep in thought. "What is the difference in people, David Ponder," the angel began, "when they hit despair? Why does one person take his own life while another moves to greatness?"

"That didn't answer my question," David replied, "but I'm not sure. I've never really thought about it."

Gabriel turned, still walking, with a mildly amused look on his face. "Think about it now," he said simply.

David shrugged. "I don't know. Maybe it's a difference in circumstances."

"Circumstances are rulers of the weak," Gabriel said, "but they are weapons of the wise. Must you be bent and flayed by every situation you encounter?" David frowned. Smiling, Gabriel pressed his point: "That is a question, David Ponder. Are your emotions and resolve controlled by circumstances?"

"No, they are not," David said firmly.

"That is correct," Gabriel nodded. "Circumstances do not push or pull. They are daily lessons to be studied and gleaned for new knowledge and wisdom. Knowledge and wisdom that is applied will bring about a brighter tomorrow. A person who is depressed is spending too much time thinking about the way things are now and not enough time thinking about how he wants things to be."

David walked on for a minute in thought, then swung his arm toward an area filled with mattresses and said, "So why are all these things here?"

Gabriel glanced at his confused pupil briefly and said, "Circumstances."

David sighed audibly. Gabriel laughed and said, "Walk this way, David Ponder."

David followed the angel down an aisle lined with telephones on one side and lumber on the other. Soon, they were back to David's starting place, the area with the photographs of children. "Have I seen it all?" David asked.

"You have seen only a tiny fraction of this facility," Gabriel answered. "A lifetime of wandering would not cover it all. And sadly, it gets bigger every day."

David stopped near the baskets of loose pictures. Reaching in, he removed the one Gabriel had placed there earlier—the one with the two children David had found so familiar. "The boy's name is Jason," Gabriel said quietly. "The girl is Julia."

David wrinkled his forehead. Still looking at the photo, he remarked, "I've always liked those names. My grandfather's name was Jason. In fact, if Jenny had been a boy, Ellen and I were going to name the baby Jason. We always said we would name our second girl Julia. We wanted several children, but we never were able to afford . . ." A cold wave of nausea swept over David. Lowering the picture slowly, he gripped the side of the large basket with his other hand to steady himself. Breathing heavily, he said, "But you already knew that, didn't you?"

"Yes," Gabriel answered.

"Why is this being done to me?"

Gabriel's eyes narrowed. "Explain yourself more clearly, please."

"Why am I seeing this now?"

"Special dispensation is allowed for a traveler to gain greater wisdom and understanding."

"I don't understand."

"Obviously."

David took a deep breath. "Am I supposed to somehow understand?"

"Everything will become clear to you."

Turning to face Gabriel, David said, "What is this place?"

Flexing the wings on his back, Gabriel took a step closer to David and swept his arms out from his sides as if to welcome an honored guest. "This, my friend, is the place that never was."

David scarcely breathed as the angel took the picture from his hands. Using it to gesture around him, Gabriel said, "This is the place where we keep all the things that were about to be delivered just as a person stopped working and praying for them. The contents of this warehouse are filled with the dreams and goals of the less courageous."

David was horrified. He turned open-mouthed, casting his eyes up and down the aisle, seeing the coats and shoes, the bicycles and blankets, and remembering the pedestal. His eyes fell again upon the photograph in Gabriel's hand. Reaching out, he asked, "May I keep it?"

"I'm sorry," the angel said, placing the picture back into

the basket. "Jason and Julia do not exist. The time for their arrival has passed. The opportunity is missed. There are no second chances."

Almost immediately, David's right hand felt for the ground. With his knees buckling, he lowered himself quickly to the floor. He didn't trust himself to stand, and so he just sat there at Gabriel's feet. He didn't scream or cry. He was past tears. He felt purged of energy, barely able even to breathe.

For what seemed like an hour or more, David sat trying to gather his senses. Gabriel stood motionless the entire time. Finally, David looked up and asked in a weak voice, "What am I supposed to learn here?"

Gabriel smiled and sat down beside David on the floor. "You must know," he began, "that in the game of life, nothing is less important than the score at halftime. The tragedy of life is not that man loses, but that he almost wins."

David shook his head slowly. "Why do we quit? Why do I quit? Why do I ease off? Why do I detour everything in my life?"

Gabriel responded instantly, "As a human, you detour and ease off because you lack understanding. You quit because you lack faith."

"Understanding about what?"

"For one thing, you do not understand that constant detours do not bring a man into the presence of greatness.

Detours do not build muscle. Detours do not provide life's lessons. Between you and anything significant will be giants in your path.

"Easing off does not make the going easier. Neither does it guide one to the desired destination. Most men ease off when the going is rough. Most slow down when the road appears treacherous. These are the times when you must feel the weight of your future on your shoulders—the throbbing, unstoppable strength of destiny coursing through your veins.

"Times of calamity and distress have always been producers of the greatest men. The hardest steel is produced from the hottest fire; the brightest star shreds the darkest night."

For a while, David was silent. He seemed deep in thought. Then as if having locked away the angel's words, he said, "Gabriel, you also mentioned that I lacked faith."

"I said those who quit lacked faith."

"You meant . . ."

"I meant your race. The human race. With only a few exceptions, you lack the faith that produces greatness." Gabriel sighed. "It was not always so. Your civilization was once alive, vibrant, productive, and borne in glory. Now look at you—a wandering, questioning pack of rebels teetering on the brink of dissolution."

"What?" David said as if he could not believe his ears.

"We are living in the most advanced age our planet has ever seen!"

Gabriel shook his head sadly. "You truly have no memory or cognitive knowledge of your history. Sometimes when I sit with our Father and watch the movements of your civilization as the time shifts, I am astounded at the arrogance I see displayed in your people. On several occasions, I have asked permission to teach you a lesson, but so far, His patience has greatly exceeded my own.

"It amuses me that you would think your civilization so advanced. There once existed a culture on earth so highly evolved as to make you look like dull children. Their mathematics, metallurgy, engineering, and architecture were far beyond what you revere today. These were people of great understanding, great wisdom, and an even greater faith."

"Why have we never heard of these people?" David asked doubtfully.

"Because most of your scientists work within a parameter of time that is far too narrow," Gabriel said. "A few of them, however, have begun to suspect that this society predated the Aztecs and Incas by more than thirty thousand of your years."

"What evidence is there of that?"

Gabriel chuckled. "Not much for you at this point. To be frank, you are too far removed from those people in terms of capacity and time. Your civilization is just now arriving at the point of recognizing the scant clues still left of their existence."

"What clues?"

Gabriel paused for a moment, then said, "The engineering of Cuencan temples, still standing in what you call South America, used stones that are rectangular in shape and weigh more than one hundred tons each. The builders of Balbek in Lebanon laid cornerstones as tall as your five-story buildings. They weigh more than six hundred tons apiece.

"In both places, and many more I might add, the andesite blocks were quarried and set together so perfectly that grout was never considered necessary. Just to cut stone to the same specifications, your engineers today require diamond-tipped, laser-guided quarry saws. And still, they can't duplicate the dimensions.

"Do you remember the Abu Simbel statues in Egypt? They are one hundred twenty feet high, one hundred forty feet wide, and weigh thirty-three tons. When an international task force of your civilization's finest engineers was assembled to save them before completion of the Aswan High Dam, they decided the only possible way to move the statues was to cut them into small sections and reassemble them on higher ground. Yet the original builders quarried the rock from a source miles away and moved it in one piece.

"Their knowledge of astronomy also far exceeded your current levels. They knew that the celestial dome is fixed—that your sun, moon, and planets rotate. They knew the exact circumference of the earth and chartered it into systems of measure around the world. Your mathematicians and engineers have now seen this in surviving buildings in South America and Europe because they incorporated the figures into their architecture. And these equations were calculated perfectly. You were able to obtain these exact mathematical values only after Sputnik circled the earth in 1957.

"Truth needs no evidence, of course." Gabriel smiled. "But since you were curious, that should give you something to consider."

For a bit, David sat still. He was almost unable to comprehend the riddle of history Gabriel had shared. He had no doubt, though, that it was true. "Why are they gone?" he finally asked. "Why did that civilization disappear?"

"For the same reasons that your civilization is in peril," Gabriel said carefully. "Arrogance, ungratefulness, and a loss of faith. Your people have reached the precipice of the same cliff in an astonishingly short time."

"Is there anything that we can do to turn back?"

"Of course," Gabriel said. "And that is precisely why you are here." Gabriel stood and helped David to his feet. Reaching into the folds of his robe, the angel drew out a small scroll. Laying it across his upturned palms, he extended it to David and said, "This decision is the final portion of the whole. Take it."

As David reached for the scroll and took it in his hand, Gabriel frowned. "I am not certain why you were selected for this great honor, David Ponder, for I am but a messenger." He paused and took a deep breath. "You are the last traveler. There will not be another. You have been given a gift that has the power to change your civilization. Everything from this moment on will key upon you.

"You will study one decision at a time, each for twenty-one days. You will read it aloud twice daily during that time. First, upon awakening, and again, as the last thing you do before sleep. You must not miss a day. Each decision will become a part of your being, buried in your heart, captured in your soul.

"You will share the gift of the decisions with others. Those who absorb and apply this wisdom will rise to greatness and inspire others to the same heights. Those who ignore the power of these scrolls might seem to prosper for a time, but do not be deceived. Their lives will be only brief illusions, and when their time is finished, they will be chained to the Mirror of Regret. There, they will spend eternity examining a reflection of the person they could have become."

Gabriel placed his hands on each side of David's face. "You have everything you need, David Ponder. You know that you are not alone. You are being guided. There will never be a reason to lose faith. The future, as you choose it, is yours. But be warned. Yours *is* a future as you choose it. Our Creator has granted you the extraordinary power of the wisdom contained in the Seven Decisions. But our Creator also grants you free will. Should you choose not to ingrain this wisdom in your life, should you choose to ignore this power, the future will be lost forever."

David took both of Gabriel's hands in his own and said, "Thank you. I will make the very most of this gift."

Gabriel smiled and stepped away, out into the middle of the aisle. "Yes, David Ponder," he said. "I believe that you will." And with that, he slowly stretched his wings over his head. Raising his arms, he swiftly drew the wings to his side. Instantly, in a thunderous rush of wind, he flew up and was gone. David moved quickly to the aisle and looked up, but he still could not see a ceiling . . . or any sign of the angel.

For a few moments, David stood there, watching and thinking. Then slowly, he began a purposeful walk. Entering the area of the pedestal, David glanced around again, as if to memorize this place and what it meant. Then he eased down onto the floor where he had felt such pain only a short time ago. He unrolled the scroll of Gabriel and read.

The Seventh Decision for Success

I will persist without exception.

Knowing that I have already made changes in my life that will last forever, today I insert the final piece of the puzzle. I possess the greatest power ever bestowed upon mankind, the power of choice. Today, I choose to persist without exception. No longer will I live in a dimension of distraction, my focus blown hither and yon like a leaf on a blustery day. I know the outcome I desire. I hold fast to my dreams. I stay the course. I do not quit.

I will persist without exception. I will continue despite exhaustion.

I acknowledge that most people quit when exhaustion sets in. I am not "most people." I am stronger than most people. Average people accept exhaustion as a matter of course. I do not. Average people compare themselves with other people. That is why they are average. I compare myself to my potential. I am not average. I see exhaustion as a precursor to victory.

How long must a child try to walk before he actually does so? Do I not have more strength than a child? More understanding? More desire? How long must I work to succeed before I actually do so? A child would never ask the question, for the answer does not matter. By persisting without exception, my outcome—my success—is assured.

I will persist without exception. I focus on results.

To achieve the results I desire, it is not even necessary that I enjoy the process. It is only important that I *continue* the process with my eyes on the outcome. An athlete does not enjoy the pain of training; an athlete enjoys the results of having trained. A young falcon is pushed from the nest, afraid and tumbling from the cliff. The pain of learning to fly cannot be an enjoyable experience, but the anguish of learning to fly is quickly forgotten as the falcon soars to the heavens.

A sailor who fearfully watches stormy seas lash his vessel will always steer an unproductive course. But a wise and experienced captain keeps his eye firmly fixed upon the lighthouse. He knows that by guiding his ship directly to a specific point, the time spent in discomfort is lessened. And by keeping his eye on the light, there never exists one second of discouragement. My light, my harbor, my future is within sight!

I will persist without exception. I am a person of great faith.

In Jeremiah, my Creator declares, "For I know the plans I have for you, plans to prosper you and not to harm you, plans to give you hope and a future." From this day forward, I will claim a faith in the certainty of my future.

Too much of my life has been spent doubting my beliefs and believing my doubts. No more! I have faith in my future. I do not look left or right. I look forward. I can only persist.

For me, faith will always be a sounder guide than reason because reason can only go so far—faith has no limits. I will expect miracles in my life because faith produces them every day. I will believe in the future that I do not see. That is faith. And the reward of this faith is to see the future that I believed.

I will continue despite exhaustion. I focus on results. I am a person of great faith.

I will persist without exception.

TEN

✛

DAVID TOOK A DEEP BREATH AND EXHALED LOUDLY.
Carefully, he rolled the scroll into a compact shape. Then,
standing, he fished the tobacco pouch from his bulging
blue jeans pocket. For a moment, David paused and ran his
fingers across the smooth fabric of Chamberlain's offhand
present to him.

He touched the two gold buttons holding the pouch
closed and marveled at the craftsmanship that had formed
an eagle on each. With the nail of his forefinger, David
traced the embroidery of crossed swords on the flap. *The
symbol of a fighting man*, he thought. *That's what I am. I am
not a quitter. I am a fighting man.* Suddenly, David smiled. "I
will persist without exception," he said aloud.

Quickly, he unfastened the buttons and squeezed the
small scroll from Gabriel into the pouch. It nestled beside
the words of a king and under the parchment from an
explorer. At a glance, David saw the crisp, white folded

stationery of two presidents, lying together as if filed carefully at the back of the pouch, beside a ragged piece of paper written in a warrior's own hand. On top of it all, David noticed as he compressed the contents and closed the pouch, were four small pages torn from the diary of a little girl.

"Thank you," he murmured as he put the pouch back in his pocket. He was overwhelmed by thoughts of the people he had met. Then David stopped. Mindful of a larger picture, he closed his eyes, bowed his head, and said the same words again. "Thank *You*."

✥

Opening his eyes, David found himself standing in a vast parking lot. He grinned and almost laughed out loud at his *lack* of astonishment. He didn't know where he was yet but was curious to note that he was not afraid or even unsure of himself. Looking around, he idly wondered if he'd ever be shocked by anything again!

It was very cold and obviously nighttime, though extensive lighting brightened the area as if it were the middle of the day. The parking lot, filled with cars, was arranged around a massive steel-and-glass arena standing several hundred yards in the distance. David, feeling strangely drawn to the building, walked toward it.

Threading his way through cars and the occasional tree that landscaped the parking lot, David felt his heart skip a beat when he realized where he was. To his left, rising almost directly over the building to which he was walking, was the Reunion Tower. In the skyline beyond it, David saw the Magnolia Building with its trademark flying red horse on top.

To the right, standing above them all was the Jolly Green Giant. That is the name, he remembered, that Jenny had given this building a week after the green argon lights had been installed to run the full length of the enormous edifice. The structure, the National Bank skyscraper, had for years been the tallest building in Dallas. David was home.

I'm back, David thought as he quickened his steps. But something didn't seem right to him. Continuing to walk toward the arena, David looked again to the Jolly Green Giant. There, no more than a mile beyond it and slightly to the east, was another even taller skyscraper that David didn't recognize. It was a beautiful white granite tower that was lit from the bottom to the top.

David stopped and slowly turned around. He examined the skyline to his north, then back to the east, south, and west. There were other new buildings as well. Frowning, David put his hands on his hips and thought, *What? Dallas has grown overnight?* Walking to the car in front of him, David narrowed his eyes. It was a red Jaguar convertible but shaped unlike any Jaguar he'd seen before. Next to the Jaguar was a burgundy Ford truck and next to it a white Lincoln. They were all different somehow, flashier maybe? A new type of paint?

He turned around again, this time counting eleven buildings that he knew for a fact were not there when . . . David cocked his head, raised his eyebrows, and smiled. He looked back at the Jaguar and laughed out loud. "I get it," he said to the car. "You are at least ten, maybe twenty years newer than anything I've ever seen.

"I'm in the future," David said to himself and began walking once again to the arena. "I'm in the future." He blew out a deep breath and shook his head. "This really ought to be interesting."

Approaching the massive building, David picked his way through a line of taxicabs and stepped up onto a broad sidewalk. There were a few people, well dressed and evidently somewhat late, hurriedly making their way through the turnstiles. David walked around for a few minutes, seeing the same scene repeated at every gate. He searched through his pockets, knowing he had no money, but thinking that just possibly a ticket might have magically appeared. *Stranger things have happened*, he thought wryly.

Okay, David thought as he stood looking up at the arena, *I have no ticket, I have no money, I'm freezing to death—what next?* Thinking that perhaps a ticket had been left in his name, David approached the ticket booth to the right of the nearest entryway and spoke to the woman behind the glass. "Excuse me," he said.

She wore a dark green sweater that accented her red hair. The lady was, David determined, in her early to mid-fifties. At the moment, with bifocals perched precariously on the end of her nose, she was speedily counting ticket stubs. As she paused to key in some numbers on her calculator, David tried again. "Excuse me, ma'am." She looked up. Opening his mouth to speak, David realized that she was smiling at a man walking up behind him.

"May I help you?" the ticket lady asked the man as David eased himself to the side. Watching the two interact, he thought, *So I can't be seen in the future either.*

David walked slowly around the arena again. Several times, from inside, he heard the thunderous ovations of what was obviously a very large number of people. He stopped briefly as a small unmarked and unlit side entrance opened a few yards in front of him.

A skinny little man emerged into the dim light. Obviously a janitor, he wore coveralls and carried a push broom. Setting the broom against the concrete wall of the building, the man shook out a ski cap, stretched it over his head, and reached into his pocket for a pipe. As a match flared, David could see more of the man's face. *Old*, he thought.

He was not consciously interested in the man's age. It was just his mind's simple acknowledgment of what his eyes were taking in. David started to walk again in a direction that took him within a few feet of the janitor. The old man glanced up as David approached and nodded, lifting his pipe.

"Good evening," he said. "You doing all right?"

"Fine, thank you," David responded automatically. Then, suddenly excited, he stopped. "Hey! You can see me?"

"Well, yeah. I can see you," the man said, somewhat confused. He placed the pipe back in his mouth. "I ain't blind yet, son. Just because I'm . . ." David had moved closer, and for the first time, the old man got a good look at David's face. "Holy cow!" he said. The pipe, unclenched from the man's teeth, fell from his mouth and rattled on the sidewalk. David quickly bent and retrieved it. "I didn't know you were . . . ," the man stammered. "I am very sorry, sir.

"Thank you very much," the man said as he took the pipe and immediately put it in his pocket. David wondered briefly if it was still lit but didn't ask. He was too curious about the way the old gentleman was acting. "Sir," the old man said, "if you don't mind me asking, are you just here checking everything out? There's a lot of people in there tonight that're mighty grateful to you, sir. My wife's not going to believe this! May I shake your hand, Mr. Ponder? My name is Jack Miller."

Shaking his hand, David asked, "You know who I am?"

"Don't worry," Jack said conspiratorially as he looked left and right. "I understand . . . and I ain't tellin' nobody. I'd want to sneak in here and see this, too, if they was all talking about me! You know, I didn't even recognize you at first. Shoot, with your hair dyed like that, you look like one of your old pictures. Say," he paused, suddenly concerned, "should you be walking around alone like this?"

David smiled slightly with his eyebrows raised. He was trying to take all this in. "I'll be fine," he said. "By the way, do you mind if I go in this door?"

Jack grinned. "Well, I reckon. You built the place. You go in any door you like! Follow me." And with that, the old man shoved his cap back into his pocket, stepped inside, and with a motion of his hand, encouraged David to stay close.

They walked through a short hall and made their way to a large tunnel that seemed to circle the arena underground. David was trying to comprehend the fact that somehow he had, or would *have*, something to do with the presence of this huge place. Striding through the tunnel, Jack waved several times at different groups of workers. They waved, nodded, or called his name in reply. "Your disguise is working great," Jack whispered loudly to David. "Don't nobody even recognize you!"

Well, David thought as he fought to suppress a laugh,

they don't recognize me because they don't see me. You, on the other hand, walking along, waving at everybody, and talking to yourself—you must be a sight to see!

"Hey," Jack said as he skidded to a stop. "I didn't even ask. Where do you want to go? Should I take you to your sky box?"

David shook his head. This was a little much. "I'd just like to wander around a bit by myself. Is that okay?"

Jack looked at David as if he had lost his mind. "Are you sure?" he said. "I can walk around with you if you want."

"No, that won't be necessary. But I really appreciate the offer. And by the way," David added as he stuck out his hand, "it has been an honor to meet you."

"Ha!" Jack snorted as he pumped David's hand vigorously. "An honor to meet me. Wait'll I tell my wife."

David left the old man and continued walking through the tunnel. Presently, he came upon an offshoot ramp that, he saw, led into the main arena. Entering the main floor, David was astonished by the sheer number of people. He had assumed by the size of the building that the seating capacity was very large, but he had, for some reason, never really imagined this place filled. There must have been four thousand people on the floor level alone.

Stepping away from the shadow of the entry ramp, David did a slow turn. He quickly noted the gigantic video screens hung from the ceiling. These were used to bring a large audience close to the action of any event. From his vantage point, David could see that they were certainly needed here. There were fully three decks completely surrounding the main floor, each seat filled to the very top. *Twenty-five thousand people in all?* David thought. *Maybe thirty thousand?*

David had heard cheers and applause several times from outside the arena and twice from the tunnel. The noise inside, he knew, would be deafening. At the moment, however, he was amazed at the virtual silence of the place. No one was walking around or even moving in the seats. No one coughed or cleared a throat. Every person in the arena was focusing every ounce of attention on the stage.

The stage, considering the enormity of its surroundings, was a relatively simple affair. It was elegantly decorated with greenery and six white Roman-style columns that rose from the stage floor to a height of approximately twenty feet. The stage was not positioned at the far end of the arena as one might have expected but, instead, was placed at the wide edge of the floor up against the first rising deck of people. The back of the platform was open so as not to obstruct the view from any angle. The effect was one of a theater-in-the-round.

It was only David's subconscious, however, that noticed anything about the stage itself. His primary attention was drawn to the center of the platform, behind the glass podium. Like the eyes of thousands of others in attendance, David's eyes were riveted to the man who was speaking.

Though standing on the opposite side of the arena, David almost directly faced the stage and was near enough to see that the speaker was a large man. He was at least three inches over six feet tall with a slim build and wore an expensive light gray double-breasted suit. The man appeared to be in his mid-forties and was ruggedly handsome—striking in a sense—his dark hair contrasting sharply with his suit. And he was crying.

David stared hard at the man, then glanced at a screen nearby to confirm in close-up what he thought he was seeing. Sure enough, there were tears rolling down this big man's face as he said, "It was only six years ago. We were out of money and out of hope. With my nine-year-old daughter lying in the hospital in critical condition, I was still working twenty-hour days, but financially, it wasn't enough. There was no longer any insurance and seemingly no help.

"As I drove my beat-up car home from work that night, I couldn't stop looking at the picture of my little girl that I had lying on the seat beside me. It was a photograph of her when she was in the third grade. I began to let my mind wander around the possibilities involved in helping my family collect the only insurance that remained, the insurance on my life."

David scarcely breathed as he listened, transfixed, to this man's story that was so eerily similar to his own.

"With money to pay the bills and make a new start," he said, the corners of his mouth quivering downward and his voice cracking, "I thought that maybe someday my wife could find a new husband—my child would have a new daddy. One who wouldn't let them down. I thought that maybe I could still give my family the life they deserved.

"I pulled off the side of the road, and as I sat there alone and thinking, I took the photograph of my child and held it in my hands. I could imagine the tubes running in and out of her body. I closed my eyes and could hear the respirator forcing air into her lungs. And suddenly, I felt ashamed!

"I felt ashamed for ever thinking of leaving her, for ever thinking of quitting. Yes, I felt ashamed. But I also felt strong again because I knew that this was a point in my life to which the First Decision truly applied. I looked at my child, my blood, my responsibility in that picture, and I said, 'The buck stops here. If you can fight that hard for your life, then surely I can fight as hard for your future!'"

David had been so unnerved by the reference to the Seven Decisions and so caught up in what this man was pouring from his heart that he was startled by the sudden and thunderous ovation. People all over the arena stood and clapped, applauding the honesty and courage of this man while he stood there, uncomfortably waiting for them to finish, tears streaming down his face.

As the applause died away and the audience settled back into their seats, David saw a single empty chair on the aisle, less than fifteen rows from the stage. Walking quickly, he moved to take the seat. He eased himself down and looked back up to the podium as the speaker continued.

"It was a simple choice really. A choice made under duress. But now, of course, our lives have been transformed—financially, emotionally, spiritually—literally transformed in every way. My family has been set free. You see, it wasn't enough that I possessed the Seven Decisions for Success or even that I understood their meaning. The moment I decided to make them a part of my life was the moment that the future of my family was secured for generations."

The man paused to drink from a glass of water. He wiped his eyes with a handkerchief and moved beside the podium. Resting his left elbow on its surface, he gestured with his right hand and said, "Think with me now. It is true that most of us have a rather limited view of the world, its history, and our own ability to affect the outcome of anything beyond our neighborhoods. In terms of personal history and legacy, we tend to restrict our concern to only three—some of us four—generations.

The vast majority of us do not even know the first names of our great-grandparents!

"Some years ago now, but well within the scope of our own generation, David Ponder bestowed upon the world the gift of the *possibility* of success for anyone. Our presence here tonight is evidence of the fruit of that gift. But I am here to challenge you to grasp a future that is far beyond your present thoughts and actions.

"There comes a time in every person's life when a decision is required. And that decision, should you make it, will have a far-reaching effect on generations yet unborn. There is a thin thread that weaves only from you to hundreds of thousands of lives. Your example, your actions, and yes, even one decision can literally change the world. Let me say that one more time. One decision, that *you* make, can literally change the world."

The speaker curiously held eye contact with the audience for several seconds after his last statement. Then he slipped back behind the podium and drank from his glass again. Replacing the glass under the podium, he regarded the crowd with a chuckle. "You know," he began, "it is an amazing feeling to be doubted by thousands of people at once!" He smiled as the crowd reacted with warm laughter of their own. "Okay, I'm going to try this again! One decision, that *you* make, can literally change the world!"

And with that, the man moved to the edge of the stage

and began animatedly telling a story. David sat spellbound as the speaker moved over every inch of the platform, involving the audience in front of him, behind him, and those at the very top of the arena. The story he told, though it had happened more than a century earlier, was absolutely accurate in its detail. David knew this to be true because he had been there.

"July second, eighteen sixty-three. It was a hot, humid day, and a schoolteacher from Maine was in the fight of his life.

"His name was Joshua Lawrence Chamberlain, formerly a professor of rhetoric from Bowdoin College, presently a thirty-four-year-old colonel in the Union army. The place? Gettysburg, Pennsylvania."

The speaker then described the dangerous situation Chamberlain's troops faced that day as they tried to hold their position against General Lee's men, the Army of Northern Virginia. After five bloody attacks from the Rebels, Chamberlain realized his troops would not be able to hold them off any longer.

The speaker explained, "More than half his regiment was dead, and many of his remaining soldiers were wounded. He was outnumbered by better than five to one, and the last skirmish had taken place on both sides of the wall, face-to-face. He didn't know how they had pushed the Rebels back down the hill. Some of his men, he later wrote, had been punching the enemy with their fists.

"As they quickly surveyed the situation, it became apparent that there were less than two bullets per man remaining. For all intents and purposes, the Twentieth Maine was out of ammunition. Glancing downhill and seeing the attackers readying themselves for a final assault, looking at what seemed to be certain defeat, certain death, Chamberlain's own officers counseled retreat. 'They outnumber us,' the men cried, 'and we have nothing with which to fight. It is hopeless. It is hopeless.'

"Joshua Chamberlain stood quietly for a moment. 'Here they come, sir,' a sergeant said urgently. Chamberlain didn't respond. He was calculating the cost of freezing, remaining, staying where he was. The cost, he determined, was essentially the same as running away.

"'Joshua!' It was his first lieutenant, his brother Tom. 'Joshua!' he screamed. 'Give an order!'

"And so he did. Chamberlain knew he had not been put on this earth to fail. But failure is the only possible result of a life that accepts the status quo. We move forward, or we die! 'Fix bayonets!' he barked. And his men looked at him as if he were crazy.

"'Excuse me, sir?' the sergeant asked, and for a moment, they all just stood there and stared.

"'They're coming!' came a yell from down the line.

"'Fix bayonets, I said!' he yelled. 'And charge!' As his men scrambled to fasten their steels, Chamberlain drew

183

his sword and jumped to the top of the wall. With the enemy now a little more than fifty yards away, he pointed his sword at them and screamed, 'Charge! Charge!' and the fighting men of the Twentieth Maine Regiment, the pride of the Army of the Potomac, poured over the wall and followed a schoolteacher into history!

"The Confederate troops, upon seeing the leader of the opposition mount the wall, immediately stopped, unsure as to what was happening. But when Chamberlain pointed his sword toward them and commanded his men to charge, they literally turned and ran. Many threw down their loaded weapons. They were certain that these were not the same soldiers they had been facing. Surely, there had been massive reinforcements. In their minds, it was *not even within the realm of possibility* that a beaten regiment would charge.

"In less than ten minutes, the ragged group of men under Chamberlain's command, without any ammunition at all at this point, captured the entire regiments of the Fifteenth Alabama and the Forty-seventh Alabama, more than four hundred men. Of course, it all happened because one man made a decision to charge.

"And one decision, that *you* make, can literally change the world."

The audience leaped out of their seats with a roar, David with them, clapping and cheering the truth, as they saw it, of the speaker's final statement. *The story of Joshua Chamberlain had inspired them, and rightly so,* David thought. It *was* an incredible event in our nation's history, and as he well knew, the speaker had been exacting in his details.

As the applause died away, David realized that the tall speaker was still on stage. In fact, he had crossed his arms and was leaning both elbows heavily on the podium. A slight smile on his face, he appeared to be patiently waiting. When the last person had settled back into his seat, and the arena was again enveloped in silence, his smile broadened. "You-all thought I was through, didn't you?"

David laughed with everyone else.

"Well, see now," he began again, "I just couldn't leave you thinking what you're thinking. And I *know,*" he said with a laugh, "what you're thinking!" He moved out to the far edge of the stage. "You're thinking, *Okay. That was a great story, but you're telling me I can change the world? Come on!* You say, 'Hey! Even Joshua Chamberlain changed the outcome of only one small part of one battle!' Oh, really? Well, consider this.

"It is an accepted fact that, at the time of the Battle of Gettysburg, the North—the Union—was losing badly. Confederate troops had taken Fort Sumter, then routed the Union army at Manassas. Lee's men won major victories at Richmond in the Battles of the Seven Days and once again at Manassas in the Second Battle of Bull

Run. The South defeated General Hooker's divisions at Chancellorsville and dealt a crushing blow to General Burnside at Fredericksburg.

"Had the South been victorious at Gettysburg, historians agree that the entire conflict would have been over by the end of the summer. The Confederate States of America were one victory away from winning the war. But they didn't win.

"The schoolteacher from Maine was awarded the Congressional Medal of Honor for his decision at Little Round Top. His commanding officers determined that the actions of this one man saved the Union army from being destroyed—this one man turned the tide of the battle. Joshua Lawrence Chamberlain turned the tide of the war.

"Do you understand what this means? If the South had won the war, there would be no America as we know it now. There would be at least two, possibly three countries existing in our place. The world would not have a country big enough and strong enough to feed the other nations of this planet. There would not be a superpower available to defend weaker societies against those that would limit their freedom. But because one ordinary man made a decision to move forward, this is a very different world we live in today.

"When Hitler swept across Europe, when Hirohito systematically invaded the islands of the Pacific, when Saddam

Hussein rolled his armies into Kuwait, there existed a *United States of America* to stand in the breach. And we were there because of one man with his back to the wall. A man who, on that hot day in July, was in fear for his very life. A man whose only option seemed to be retreat. Ladies and gentlemen, the world as it exists today is largely the result of a decision to charge—one decision made by a schoolteacher more than a hundred years ago!

"Don't you *ever* think that you can't change things! You can! You can! One decision, that *you* make, can change the world!"

Once more the entire arena was on its feet. David was stunned. As he clapped, he couldn't get over the incredible chain of events that had been set in motion by one man. *What had happened to Chamberlain?* he wondered. As the crowd quieted and resettled, the speaker continued, and David found out.

"It is a fact that people follow a man who simply says, 'Follow me.' By taking leadership, ironically, a person *deserves* leadership. As you lead others to success and a life of their dreams, the life you seek and deserve will be revealed unto you.

"Joshua Chamberlain made a decision that changed our world, yes, but his decision also held personal rewards. He led successful campaigns until the end of the war. He was cited by our government four separate times for bravery in action and was promoted to brigadier general for heroism at Petersburg, this by special order of Ulysses S. Grant. Then, only a few months later, for heroism at Five Forks, he was promoted to major general.

"Among all Union officers, President Abraham Lincoln chose Chamberlain to have the honor of accepting the Confederate surrender at Appomattox. There, he stunned the world with a show of forgiveness and respect as he ordered his troops to attention, saluting General Robert E. Lee and the defeated South.

"Back home, in Maine, Chamberlain was elected governor in what is, to this day, the largest majority in the history of the state. He was reelected three times until finally, he stepped down and accepted a role of leadership at his alma mater, as president of Bowdoin College.

"Incidentally, an interesting benefit of a person's decision to charge, one that has been somewhat overlooked by scholars and historians, is the presence of a hedge of thorns. Mentioned first in the Bible, a hedge of thorns is the divine protection placed upon a person who is destined to make a difference. Until you have accomplished what you were put here to do, you will not—you cannot—be harmed. Joshua Chamberlain, on that hill in Pennsylvania, with his decision to charge not yet made and all his victories before him, was wrapped in the protection of a hedge of thorns."

The dark-haired speaker reached into the inside pocket of his jacket and brought out a small piece of paper. Holding it up for everyone to see, he said, "I have here a copy of a letter addressed to the Honorable Governor Joshua L. Chamberlain. It arrived at the statehouse several years after the war." He unfolded the page, smoothed it out on top of the podium, and read,

"Dear Sir: I want to tell you of a little passage in the Battle of Round Top, Gettysburg, concerning you and me, which I am now glad of. Twice in that fight I had your life in my hands. I got a safe place between two rocks, and drew bead fair and square on you. You were standing in the open behind the center of your line, full exposed. I knew your rank by your uniform and actions, and I thought it a mighty good thing to put you out of the way. I rested my gun on the rock and took steady aim. I started to pull the trigger, but some queer notion stopped me. Then I got ashamed of my weakness and went through the same motions again. I had you, perfectly certain. But that same queer something shut right down on me. I couldn't pull the trigger, and, gave it up—that is, your life. I am glad of it now, and hope you are. Yours truly, A Member of the Fifteenth Alabama."

Slowly, the speaker refolded the paper as chills ran through the audience. He tucked it back into his jacket pocket and moved to the very edge of the stage. David felt the man look directly at him as he said softly, "You, too, at this very moment are living under the protection of a hedge of thorns. You might feel fear, but it is an illusion. Until you have accomplished what you were put on this earth to do, you will not—you cannot—be harmed."

Then he held his arms up in a broad gesture to the crowd. "My friends, it all comes down to this. Your story, your circumstances, your timing may not be as dramatic as those of Joshua Chamberlain, but the stakes are exactly the same. There comes a time in every person's life when a decision is required. And that decision, should you make it, will have a far-reaching effect on generations yet unborn. There is a thin thread that weaves from only you to hundreds of thousands of lives. Your example, your actions, and yes, even one decision that you make *will* literally change the world.

"A decision . . . to charge." He paused. "So do it. Change your life. Change your family's future. Change the world. Charge." The audience didn't breathe. The tall man held them with his eyes. In a softer voice, he said, "Charge." Again a pause, then a whisper, "Charge."

For what seemed an eternity, but in reality must have been only several seconds, no one moved. Then in an explosion of sound both sudden and deafening, thousands rose as one, not only cheering this man who had brought a message of hope and instruction, but also celebrating their future. The applause continued on and on until the speaker, whom David had watched disappear into the tunnel entrance, returned to the stage. He waved, acknowledging their appreciation. David smiled as the man's eyebrows raised in apparent surprise at the intensity of the ovation. He waved again, turning in all directions, and then quickly was gone.

There were a few brief announcements over the public address system, but the evening, apparently, was over. David stood to the side as the lines of men and women filed out. He looked carefully at their faces and saw determination, tears of understanding and relief, and a peace that can come only from certainty.

In less than thirty minutes, the arena was empty. After one last look, David entered the tunnel, found an exit, and walked out into the frigid night.

Walking aimlessly along the sidewalk, David watched the red taillights of cars as they jockeyed for space exiting the parking lot. He looked again at the skyline of the city, so familiar and yet so different. It occurred to David as he strolled along that he didn't have any idea as to his next move. *Am I supposed to meet someone else?* he wondered. *Look for something? Go somewhere?*

Without any conscious purpose, David veered off the sidewalk and into the parking lot. The night air was clear, and though he was cold, he felt well physically. *In fact,* David thought, *I've never felt better.* He surveyed the huge empty space; black asphalt and white lines seemed to continue forever.

It had been well over an hour since the event had ended, and all the cars were gone—except one. There, straight in front of him sixty or seventy yards away, in the shadows of a tree, sat one car. David shook his head and walked directly to it. It was one very familiar car. Small, mostly faded silver except for the right fender, which was black. It was his two-door Dodge Colt. "Uh-huh," David said aloud as he approached. "And I'll bet the heater and brake lights *still* don't work."

The car was open, and not surprisingly, the keys swung from the ignition. David squeezed himself into the tiny car, noticing the black windbreaker he'd thrown into the backseat . . . when? This morning? It was too confusing to think about. He turned the key, and the little engine sputtered to life. David reached above the sun visor, and yes, there was his watch with its cheap gold band stretched around his wallet. "Wow!" he said and smiled as he put the watch on his wrist and placed the wallet in the passenger seat beside him.

So where to? he thought as the car idled loudly. Looking around, he saw that the beautiful white skyscraper he'd noticed earlier was framed perfectly in the right rear window. "Okay," David said softly as he put the Colt into gear.

He made a series of turns out of the parking lot and soon

was headed in the general direction of the white tower. Every now and then, David could see it appear between other buildings and through trees. It was easy to locate. After all, it was the tallest building in the city.

When he found the last street that led to the object of his brief search, David stopped the car. He stared at the street sign but wasn't sure he could believe his eyes. He glanced around. It was well past midnight. There were no other cars around just then, and so he opened his door and got out. He quickly walked to the corner and peered closely up at the sign. Silently, he turned around and walked back to the car. He eased it into gear, took a deep breath, and made a right onto David Ponder Boulevard.

There, directly in front of him, was the enormous white building. Oak trees lined the boulevard on either side, and as David got closer, he was awed by a majestic fountain spraying water high into the air near the main entrance. He found himself unable to take his eyes off the architectural masterpiece, and when he reached it, he simply stopped the car by the curb and got out.

David slowly wandered across an open expanse of gray rough-hewn marble. It covered an area of at least thirty yards from the street and was laid around the entire circumference of the structure. At night, because of the reflection of the building and its ambient light, the dark stone looked wet.

He walked to a series of five revolving doors at the main entrance. They were locked. Easing to the right, David put his face to the glass and looked inside, holding his hands around his eyes to shield the glare. The whole main floor seemed to be a reception area, a lobby, that was capped by its own dome at about the fifth level. Huge palms, at least twenty-five feet tall, were growing in colossal earthenware pots. They were arranged between the doors of six glass elevators, which were all poised at the bottom, waiting for their morning passengers.

Great tapestries hung on the walls from the ceiling to the lush carpet below. The centerpiece, in the middle of this spectacular main floor, was a waterfall cascading more than forty feet from a single granite boulder. It fell into a koi pond that wrapped around the elevator shaft and ended at the foot of a large stone concierge desk that looked as if it would require six to ten receptionists. Carved into the stone, on the front of the desk facing the entrance, were the words: PONDER INTERNATIONAL.

David moved away from the glass. He was not really surprised. Excited, yes, but not surprised. He was coming to grips with the reality of his successful future. *There is a thin thread that weaves from only you to hundreds of thousands of lives*, David remembered. *Well*, he thought, *there are a few of those lives working in this building.*

David moved back to his car, stopping briefly by the

fountain. A sign there read: "Coins donated in this fountain are used in support of the Jenny Ponder Zoological Gardens, City of Dallas." He smiled and went to the car.

For a while, David drove randomly and found the streets mostly empty and the city very quiet. Finding himself near the interstate, without really thinking about it, he turned onto the freeway. He drove for more than an hour to nowhere in particular. He spotted the Ellen Ponder Children's Hospital from an overpass, exited, and sat in its parking lot for several minutes.

David drove past the empty and boarded-up building that had been Marshall's Hardware. Apparently, it had been closed for years. As if on automatic pilot, he steered into his neighborhood and saw the name "McClain" on his old mailbox. The dogwoods he and Jenny had planted beside the house had grown as high as the roof.

He saw the church they attended, passed Jenny's elementary school, and noted with a shake of his head that the chemical plant where he'd worked for so many years had changed ownership again.

Before long, with no specific intent, David found himself back on the interstate headed out of the city. He was, he knew, a very different man. When he took the Grayton exit, he was only vaguely aware that he'd been there before. His mind whirled with thoughts of Truman and his piercing, clear blue eyes. He glanced at the speedometer. It read seventy.

He remembered Solomon's throne and smiled faintly. The king had said it was only a chair!

There were no other vehicles in sight. The headlights of the little car burst through the darkness like cannon fire on a Pennsylvania hilltop. He pressed harder on the accelerator and saw certainty in a sea captain's face as the man watched the horizon. Eighty . . . eighty-five. Anne. That dear, sweet little girl. "Papa says, 'Fear is a poor chisel with which to carve out tomorrow.'"

As he flew over hills and around curves, David became oblivious to his speed. *I spoke to Abraham Lincoln,* he thought. *He spoke to me.* "The secret of forgiveness costs nothing and is worth millions." David's mind was racing at a furious pace. "You are the last traveler," the angel said. "You have been given a gift that has the power to change your civilization. Everything from this moment on will key upon you."

At that instant, David Ponder's destiny intersected with an icy bridge. Covering a small stream, the bridge was still no more than fifty feet long, and the same black ice sent the speeding car careening into a spin. Tires screeching, David's car bounced off the guardrail as he crossed the short bridge and found that he remained on the highway.

Interestingly, David did *not* fight desperately for control as the car fishtailed from side to side and finally swerved off the road. He watched the scene unfold from inside the vehicle as if in slow motion. He wanted to remember everything, especially as the car careened helplessly toward a giant oak tree. With his remaining conscious thought, David gripped the steering wheel and closed his eyes. He heard the speaker in the arena say, "Until you have accomplished what you were put on this earth to do, you will not—you cannot—be harmed!"

And then . . . nothing.

ELEVEN

✛

"HONEY? DAVID?" DAVID'S VISION WAS BLURRY AS
he tried to focus on the person in front of him. "David, it's
Ellen. Can you hear me?"

He heard another voice, a man. "It may take some time,
Mrs. Ponder." Everyone sounded so far away.

"Daddy, I love you." Jenny?

"David. This is Ellen. Sweetheart, I'm right here."

David felt his wife's hand on his face as his eyes cleared
somewhat. He could see her hand now and her face. Her
beautiful face. "Ellen," he managed to rasp out. Oh, brother,
he had a headache! "Ellen," he said again and tried to
reach for her.

"I'm here, honey," she said as she pushed his arm down.
"Please don't move." She had tears running down her face.
"David, you've been in an accident. You're in the hospital."

"Don't cry," David said groggily. "We're going to be
okay." He began to sit up.

Ellen gently forced him back. "Yes, honey," she said. "You're going to be fine, but you have a concussion. David, please be still."

His vision and hearing seemed to come and go, closer and farther, softer and louder. "No," he said with an effort. "I don't mean me. I mean *us*. We're going to be okay, our family. Where's Jenny?"

"She's right here."

"I'm here, Daddy," she said as she came to the bed. "I love you."

"I love you too. How is your throat?"

"Hurts some, but not horrible."

David reached up to touch her silky hair. "We will fix your throat, baby. I promise. Ellen?" He called his wife's name more loudly than he'd intended, and it startled everyone in the room.

"I'm here, David. I'm right here." She was still holding his hand and had not moved from his side.

"Ellen, we are going to be okay. I know things now. I went to places that . . ."

And suddenly, he woke up. In a matter of several seconds, David's head cleared and his vision sharpened. He looked around and, seeing his wife, daughter, and a short man in a white coat huddled over him, asked, "Where am I?"

"You're in the hospital, honey," Ellen answered. "You were in an accident."

"Am I . . . ?"

"You will recover, Mr. Ponder." The short man moved forward. "I'm Doctor Green. You are a very lucky man, sir."

"I hit a tree."

"Yes, you did," the doctor replied, "And actually, that is a very significant sign in our favor, the fact that you remember anything at all. You have suffered a severe concussion. Do you remember anything else?"

"I had been at the arena."

Ellen furrowed her eyebrows. "No, honey," she said. "You had been at work. David, why were you so far out of town?"

The doctor placed his hand on her shoulder. "Mrs. Ponder," he interrupted, "there will be quite a few jumbled thoughts for a while. Confusing dreams, misplaced conversations." He smiled at David and shrugged. "That is one nasty lick to the head you have, but all in all, I can honestly say, I've never seen anything like it. The skull is not fractured. The paramedics who brought you in said you'd been thrown from the car, and yet so far, except for the concussion, we haven't found so much as one broken bone. Yes, sir. I'd say that you are one extremely lucky man."

As the doctor went on about what to expect as he healed and which medicines would be prescribed and why and how long he could plan on staying in the hospital, David watched his wife and child. He was a lucky man, he knew, but a curious disappointment settled over him like a fog. A dream. It had all been a dream. A confusing dream, the doctor had called it.

". . . and of course, we just take our time with these things," the doctor was finishing. "So, why don't we leave for a little while and let your dad get some rest?" he said to Jenny.

"I'll take Jenny home, honey," Ellen said. "Mom and Dad have come in to help so they're at the house. As soon as I drop her off, I'll be back." Ellen carefully kissed David on the cheek and turned to leave. "I love you," she added.

David saw that the doctor had already slipped out of the room. A tear rolled down his cheek. "I love you, too, Ellen. I'm sorry for all this."

She moved back to the bed and positioned herself over him so that she could look directly into his eyes. "David, you have nothing to be sorry about. Jenny and I love you and trust you and want you back home. Do you remember telling me a few minutes ago that our family was going to be okay?" She smiled. "Well, you were right."

David lay alone in the small hospital room. Ellen had kissed him again before she left. He listened to the click of her heels and the squeak of Jenny's tennis shoes fade away down the hall. *A dream*, he thought. He sighed deeply.

He wasn't sleepy. His body throbbed and his head still hurt, but he wasn't sleepy. He looked above the sink beside the bed to find the source of a quiet beeping. It was a monitor of some kind. On the other side of the bed, a tube snaked its way from a plastic bag of solution hanging on a pole down to his arm, where, David was certain, a needle meant for some large animal had been mistakenly inserted into him.

There was a small cot over in the corner. Had Ellen been sleeping there? How long had he been here? A television was attached to the wall across from him. There was an extra door that led to what he assumed was the bathroom, and except for a chair under the television, that was it. *Nothing to look at,* he thought. So he looked at the ceiling.

It had all seemed so real. He had been there! He just *knew* he'd been in Potsdam. He had been in Amsterdam and with Columbus on the *Santa Maria.* He hadn't been in a car accident—he'd been in two! But no one would ever believe him, David knew, and considering his surroundings, he wasn't sure he believed it himself.

Anyway, David thought, *it wasn't the experience that was important, was it? What did I learn? Even if it had been a dream, did the Seven Decisions for Success have less value?* David smiled when he realized that by concentrating just a bit, he could recall the key phrases and basic philosophy of each principle.

Not trusting himself to remember them for long, David

found a pen and writing pad on the small table beside him. He raised himself into a sitting position and wrote:

1. The buck stops here. I am responsible for my past and my future.

2. I will seek wisdom. I will be a servant to others.

3. I am a person of action. I seize this moment. I choose now.

4. I have a decided heart. My destiny is assured.

5. Today I will choose to be happy. I am the possessor of a grateful spirit.

6. I will greet this day with a forgiving spirit. I will forgive myself.

7. I will persist without exception. I am a person of great faith.

David reread what he had written and nodded his head. He was tired. He would work more on this later—remember more later. He placed the pen and paper on the table next to him. David intended to reconstruct every decision and commit them to his heart as Gabriel had told him to do. He took a deep breath, sighed, and corrected himself . . . as he had dreamed Gabriel had told him to do.

No matter, David thought as he stared at the ceiling. *My family will be fine. Our future is assured. I will make it so.* The pebbled surface of the ceiling, reflecting tiny points of light, reminded David of stars. He closed his eyes. Maybe he was sleepy, after all.

Just as he was about to drift off, David heard the slight whoosh of the door opening. A nurse entered. "I am so sorry," she said. "I didn't mean to wake you."

"No problem," David said. "I wasn't really asleep."

"You just keep resting then," she said kindly. "I'll leave this right here and get out of your way." She had a dark plastic bag in her hand, and she moved to place it in the chair.

"What is that?" David asked.

"Personal effects. Wallet and stuff. Shoes. Everything you were wearing when you had your accident. They brought it up from Emergency."

"Could I have the bag over here, please?" David asked. "I'd like to put on my watch."

"I can do that," the nurse said as she put the bag on the edge of the bed beside David. "And your watch is in here," she smiled. "We have to inventory everything, you know, and I saw it myself."

"Thank you," David said as she left the room.

He opened the bag and pulled out his shoes. His socks were stuffed in one and his boxers in the other. They were resting on his sweatshirt and jeans, which someone had neatly folded. David dropped the shoes and clothes to the floor on the other side of the bed.

David's wedding band had fallen out with the clothes and was resting on the white sheet. He placed it on his finger and reached back into the bag for his watch, found it, and stretched the band onto his wrist. His key ring was in the bag. And his wallet. *Wasn't my wallet on the seat beside me?* David tried to remember. *Oh, well,* he thought. *Thanks to someone for getting it out of the car.* He put the wallet on the table.

Lifting the plastic bag to move it from the bed, David felt a slight heaviness. Realizing he'd missed something, he stopped and reopened it. At first, he didn't see anything. But there, stuck in the corner, was a small dark object, almost the color of the plastic bag.

Scarcely daring to breathe, David felt his heart pound as he reached through the folds of plastic and removed a small tobacco pouch. Tears welled up in his eyes as he held it up in the light.

It was navy blue and had been sewn from stout cloth, but the rough treatment it had received had worn the pouch to a moleskin softness. It was beaten and threadbare, but it was still handsome, regal in a sense, the possession of an officer. The two gold buttons that closed the flap were metal, engraved with the image of an eagle. And there, just above the buttons, embroidered on the flap, were crossed swords—the symbol of a fighting man.

ACKNOWLEDGMENTS

I WOULD LIKE TO THANK POLLY, MY WIFE AND BEST friend, for the patience shown during endless conversations about this project; David Brokaw for his support and belief in me; Scott Jeffrey for his creative presentation strategies; Mike Hyatt, Pamela Clements, Blythe McIntosh, and the team at Thomas Nelson who didn't just contract for a book, but caught a vision! Thanks to Jenny Baumgartner for her editing skills, and the people skills she used on me as she edited! An extra measure of gratitude to Belinda Bass for the extra time and care she took in designing the cover.

Special thanks go to Sandi Dorff, Isabel Garcia, Alex McCurley, Susie White, Paula Tebbe, and Julie Plato—the people who, in support of my life, made this book possible. And finally, a very special thanks to Danita Allen, who shaped the story and my words from the beginning.

READER'S GUIDE

✦

THIS READER'S GUIDE WAS CREATED TO FACILITATE
a better understanding of the life changing principles
expressed in *The Traveler's Gift*. These questions may be
used for group discussion or personal reflection. It is the
author's hope that your exploration of the Seven Decisions
and the inspirational teachings will lead to an extraordi-
narily fulfilled life and the desire to share the Decisions
with others.

+‡+

General Questions

1. How does the book exemplify the differences between people who encounter despair? What have your experiences been like?

2. Why is it important that David visited the historical figures during crucial moments in history?

3. Andrews incorporates facts and details about American history into the book. Why is it important that successful people have more than a "limited view" of history? How does historical knowledge lead to success in the future?

4. How does Andrews explore the importance of associations with other people? How are relationships integrally connected to wisdom? How do the relationships between David and the seven historical figures support this point?

5. What is the significance of the title? What importance does time travel have in the story? How does time travel change David's life?

✤

GENERAL QUESTIONS ABOUT
the Seven Decisions for Success

1. What do you think Andrews accomplishes by placing the *Seven Decisions* at the end of each visit with a historical figure?

2. How do these documents contribute to your understanding of David Ponder's journey?

3. How different would the book be had the historical characters visited David in his present time, similar to Scrooge being visited by ghosts in Charles Dickens' *A Christmas Carol*?

4. What would have been the affect of the *Seven Decisions* had David not become distinguished and wealthy at the end of the book? Are his fame and fortune a fulfillment of the *Seven Decisions* or merely a by-product?

✜

THE MAIN CHARACTER: DAVID PONDER

1. The book begins during a crossroads in David's life. How does David's mindset about his personal crisis change by the end of the book?

2. Discuss the criticisms the seven historical characters make about David. Do you think they should have been tougher on him? Why or why not?

3. How did your opinion of David change throughout the book?

4. David is locked in a constant struggle with himself. In what ways does his behavior echo the struggles faced by the historical figures in the novel? What types of consequences can these conflicts have?

5. What is David's attitude toward the past? Toward the future? How are these attitudes changed by the end of the book?

6. In what ways is David an "Everyman" who is experiencing a journey applicable to all humans?

✛

GENERAL QUESTIONS
ABOUT THE HISTORICAL FIGURES

1. Talk about the theme of leadership in the book. Which historical figures talk about leadership, and how do those comments directly relate to the person speaking?

2. What overall definition of leadership does Andrews offer?

3. The historical figures are bridges between life and death, between past, present, and future. How does this define their messages to David?

4. Each historical figure personally embodies a particular decision. Having broader knowledge of their lives beyond this book, what evidence do you see that any of them also included the other decisions in their lives?

✥

Chapter Three:
HARRY S. TRUMAN

The First Decision:
The buck stops here.

I will not let my history control my destiny.

1. President Harry Truman tells David, "You have chosen the pathway to your present destination. The responsibility for your situation is yours." Do you believe that an individual's present state is solely determined by personal choice and responsibility? Why or why not?

2. Truman says, "Our thinking creates a pathway to success or failure." Can you remember a particular instance when your thinking created success? Can you remember a particular instance when your thinking led to failure? Describe these instances and what you've learned from them.

3. Why does Andrews consider challenges a gift?

✛

Chapter Four:
KING SOLOMON

The Second Decision:
I will seek wisdom.

God moves mountains to create the opportunity
of His choosing. It is up to you to be ready
to move yourself.

1. King Solomon says, "We, as humans, are always in a process of change. Therefore, we might as well guide the direction in which we change." How will the decision to "seek wisdom" help you guide the direction in which you change?

2. Why does Andrews consider the people with whom we associate to be a critical component to seeking wisdom?

3. What point is King Solomon making when he directs David to understand that "serving is a way we can place value on one another"? He says, "A wise man is a server." Why?

✛

Chapter Five:
JOSHUA CHAMBERLAIN

The Third Decision:
I am a person of action.

*Many people move out of the way for a person on
the run; others are caught up in his wake.*

1. In what ways is Joshua Chamberlain's tobacco
   pouch symbolic? What does the pouch look
   like? Why is the physical description repeated
   throughout the book?

2. The book opens with a quotation by Joshua
   Chamberlain, an obscure figure in American
   history. How does this quote set the stage for
   the book?

3. Why do you think Andrews chose to begin
   with a quote by Chamberlain instead of one by
   the other historical characters in the book?

✛

Chapter Six:
CHRISTOPHER COLUMBUS

The Fourth Decision:
I have a decided heart.

*Criticism, condemnation, and complaint are
creatures of the wind. They come and go
on the wasted breath of lesser beings
and have no power over me.*

1. Through Columbus, what does Andrews say about the world's perception of madness and its definition of reality?

2. When does persistence toward a goal become insanity and when is it an admirable trait for success?

3. In what ways are Columbus' passion and decided heart essential to his leadership?

✛

Chapter Seven:
ANNE FRANK

The Fifth Decision:
Today I will choose to be happy.

Our very lives are fashioned by choice. First we make choices. Then our choices make us.

1. What do you think the pictures hanging in Anne Frank's room represent?

2. Is Anne's life considered a success in this book? Why or why not?

3. Why does Anne consider her personality, her habits, even her speech to be determined by choices she makes?

✦

Chapter Eight:
ABRAHAM LINCOLN

The Sixth Decision:
I will greet this day with a forgiving spirit.

You will find that God rarely uses a person whose main concern is what others are thinking.

1. President Abraham Lincoln tells David that the key to his future is forgiveness. Why is forgiveness such an important step for David at this point in his life? Whom does he need to forgive?

2. How would you describe the importance of the *Decision of Forgiveness* when compared to the other Decisions?

3. Why does Lincoln encourage David to become a "lighthouse" of personal growth and power?

✛

Chapter Nine:
GABRIEL

The Seventh Decision:
I will persist without exception.

Reason can only be stretched so far, but faith has no limits. The only limit to your realization of tomorrow is the doubt you hold fast today.

1. David visits the archangel Gabriel in "the place that never was," a large celestial warehouse that holds the lost dreams of humanity. Why is it important that David's last visit with a historical figure occurs in this place?

2. What does he learn about circumstances and opportunities from Gabriel?

3. Talk about the treatment of fear in the book. What is the relationship between fear and success? Why does Gabriel say that faith and fear are the same?

✛

QUESTIONS
FOR PERSONAL REFLECTION

1. How will what you've read in this book help you during you own times of crises?

2. *The Traveler's Gift* underscores the importance of rising above the opinions of others. How do your self-perceptions dictate your success? What advice does David receive for differentiating between wise counsel and criticism? How can you apply this advice to your life right now?

3. Andrews gives a prescribed method for absorbing the *Seven Decisions*—reading each decision aloud, morning and night, for twenty-one days and sharing the decisions with others. Is this something you can implement in your life? If you did, how could it change your future? How could it change others' futures?

4. In what ways can you use the life lessons in *The Traveler's Gift* to encourage and change the lives of others?

5. Why might *The Traveler's Gift* be a vital book for our country/planet at this time?

6. Each historical character refers to faith in some way. What do you think Andrews is suggesting about the connection between faith and success? How does the book's overall message define success as a combination of personal initiative and divine motivation?

✤

Final Bonus Questions

1. Dreams are a recurring motif in the book. How does each historical figure emphasize the importance of dreams as vehicles for success? What is the purpose of dreams? At the end, David briefly worries that his journey has all been a dream. How is this significant to the meaning of dreams?

2. At the end of the book, the speaker in the arena says, "Until you have accomplished what you were put on earth to do, you will not—you cannot—be harmed." How is this concept of a "hedge of thorns," or divine protection, fitting to the journey David has taken?

BIBLIOGRAPHY

America's Civil War. Leesburg, VA: Primedia Enthusiast Publications History Group, January, 1999.

Becker, Walt. *Link*. New York: William Morrow and Company, Inc. NY, 1998.

Chamberlain, Joshua Lawrence. *Bayonet Forward, My Civil War Reminiscences*. Gettysburg, PA: Stan Clark Military Books, 1994.

Chamberlain, Joshua Lawrence. *Through Blood and Fire at Gettysburg*. Gettysburg, PA: Stan Clark Military Books, 1994.

Compton's Interactive Encyclopedia. Cambridge, MA: The Learning Company.

Desjardin, Thomas A. *Stand Firm Ye Boys From Maine*. Gettysburg, PA: Thomas Publications, 1995.

Dyson, John. *Westward with Columbus*. New York: Simon and Schuster, Inc. New York: 1991.

Encarta. Redmond, Washington: Microsoft Corporation, 1997.

Frank, Anne. *The Diary of a Young Girl*. New York: Doubleday, 1995.

Gies, Miep. *Anne Frank Remembered*. New York: Simon and Schuster, Inc., 1987.

Hobson, Alan. *One Step Beyond*. Banff Alberta Canada: Altitude Publishing, 1992.

Mason, John. *An Enemy Called Average*. Tulsa, OK: John Mason, 1990.

Mason, John. *Conquering An Enemy Called Average*. Tulsa, OK: Insight International, 1996.

Mason, John L. *You're Born an Original Don't Die a Copy*. Altamonte Springs, FL: Insight International, 1993.

McCullough, David. *Truman*. New York: Simon and Schuster, Inc., 1992.

Muller, Melissa. *Anne Frank—the Biography*. New York: Henry Holt and Company, 1998.

Persico, Joseph E. *My Enemy My Brother, Men and Days of Gettysburg*. New York: Macmillan Publishing Company, 1977.

Phillips, Donald T. *Lincoln On Leadership*. New York: Warner Books, 1992.

Pullen, John J. *The Twentieth Maine*. Dayton, OH: Morningside House, Inc., 1957.

Shaara, Michael. *The Killer Angels*. New York: The Ballantine Publishing Group, 1974.

The Living Bible. Wheaton, IL: Tyndale House Publishers, Inc., 1971.

Wills, Garry. *Lincoln at Gettysburg, The Words That Remade America*. New York: Touchstone, 1992.

World Book Encyclopedia. Chicago, IL: World Book, Inc., 1993.

ABOUT
THE AUTHOR

✠

HAILED BY A *NEW YORK TIMES* REPORTER AS "someone who has quietly become one of the most influential people in America," Andy Andrews is a best-selling novelist, speaker, and consultant for the world's largest corporations and organizations. He has spoken at the request of four different United States presidents and recently addressed members of congress and their spouses. Zig Ziglar said, "Andy Andrews is the best speaker I have ever seen." Andy is the author of the *New York Times* bestsellers *The Noticer* and *How Do You Kill 11 Million People?* He lives in Orange Beach, Alabama, with his wife, Polly, and their two sons.

JOIN ANDY'S VIP E-MAIL LIST FOR FREE ACCESS TO:

- *Exclusive Online Resources*
- *Weekly Blog and Podcast Content from Andy*
- *Special Promotions*
- *and More*

Go to AndyAndrews.com to join for free!
To book Andy for corporate events,
go to the website or call

(800) 726-ANDY (2639)

The SEVEN DECISIONS

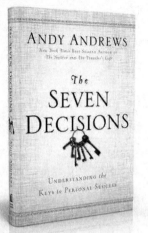

You've read *The Traveler's Gift*...

Now here's how to take what you've learned and generate Massive Action in your life!

Consider *The Seven Decisions* to be an Owner's Manual of sorts for *The Traveler's Gift*. It will take you step-by-step through implementing each of the seven decisions in different areas of your life.

Change can happen in an instant. The question is . . . are you ready for it? If the answer is "Yes," then *The Seven Decisions* is for you!

GET OUT OF YOUR RUT

WITH FREE VIDEO TRAINING
FROM ANDY ON THE SEVEN DECISIONS

Go to **GuidedTraveler.com** to watch a free 3-part video series on how to use the wisdom of extraordinary people to transform your life.

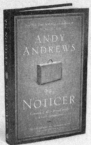
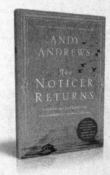